A HOUSE WITH FOUR ROOMS

A GUIDE TO LIVING AN INTENTIONAL LIFE WITH PHYSICAL, MENTAL, EMOTIONAL, AND SPIRITUAL WELLBEING

LISA MCGRATH

OLIVER GOLDEN PUBLISHING

DOWNLOAD YOUR GIFT EBOOK: THE POWER OF EVERY DAY ROUTINES!

Congratulations on making YOURSELF a priority!

That's what the philosophy of *A House With Four Rooms* is all about: making sure you do something daily for your physical, mental, emotional, and spiritual wellbeing.

And when you do...you discover your purpose, align your goals, and live an Intentional Life.

You'll find yourself capable of achieving all of your personal and professional goals.

https://www.lisamcgrath.me/offers/YUFefz2S

If you have any questions, please reach out to me...I'm happy to help!

In love and light,

Lisa

~

To those I call family...with love and light.

CONTENTS

INTRODUCTION

A HOUSE WITH FOUR ROOMS

Early in my adulthood, I learned from reading a book by author Rumer Godden the Indian Proverb that says "Everyone should think of themselves as a house with four rooms: physical, mental, an emotional, and a spiritual. Most of us tend to live in one room most of the time, but unless we go into every room every day, even if only to keep it aired, we are not a complete person." Much of my life I've referred back to this proverb, whether to remind myself or sharing its wisdom with others; as a teacher, I've shared it with many students over the years.

My search for a deeper meaning and purpose in my life began as a little girl because I was thrust into adulthood at an early age and didn't have the normal upbringing of my peers. I lived on my own and sought out ways *to live a more meaningful life.*

I've read many books and often returned to my interest in the Simplicity Movement to find balance in my everyday life. I've enjoyed books such as *The Circle of Simplicity by* Cecile Andrews and Joe Domingues and Vicki Robin's book *Your Money or Your Life: Transforming Your Relationship with Money and Achieving Financial*

Independence; I've been a huge follower of Wayne Dyer, Louise Hay, and Cheryl Richardson; and I've learned a lot from life experience.

When my life gets overwhelming and time escapes me, I tend to fall back, reflect, and make another list; I'm a list person. I make lists for almost everything, and like many people, I get a thrill crossing off items on my lists. But there are plenty of times that my lists are unreasonable and it is nearly impossible for me to get everything accomplished. I get overwhelmed and the "self-talk" becomes negative and I need to get myself back on track. It's at these times that I need the simplicity and lessons of this Indian Proverb.

I have used this proverb when I counsel others in my coaching programs and engage in it for myself, but lately, I've realized that I have not spent enough quality time in each of my rooms.

David Wann, author of *Simple Prosperity: Finding Real Wealth in a Sustainable Lifestyle,* states, "All the baggage we carry (physical, emotional, and psychological) is getting very heavy; it's time for us to reinvent a more moderate economy based on how nature actually works and what humans actually need" *(24).*

So, to create balance and a commitment to myself, I embarked on a more formal version of my practice by developing PATHS to journey down and learn more about and it became a sort of *pilgrimage to self* as I learned self-awareness, forgiveness, mindset, gratitude, and so many more life management skills.

I have thought of myself as *A House With Four Rooms* since learning about the proverb, and even more so lately. This book engages in my perspective, connecting in life, and nourishing the moments; it's my guide of growing, managing, and sustaining a lifestyle.

According to Wann, "When we understand who we are and what we want, we have a greater sense of clarity and direction" *(28).*

If you are like me, you want your lifestyle to reflect the complete person you want to be, so we will begin with examining our values, discovering our purpose, and defining our goals; we'll also make a visit to each of our four rooms. Remember, you might not spend a great deal of time in each of the rooms each day, but you must at least go in and open a window to "air" it out.

CHAPTER 1

EXTRAORDINARY MOMENTS

here have been many times that I have faced crossroads in life, and I struggled to make decisions for my highest and best good. I often put the needs of others before my own or I was paralyzed by fear. Even though I haven't always followed it, I'm fortunate I have a divine inner compass. I believe we all have an inner compass, but we all don't have immediate access to it if we haven't honed the practice of using it. I also believe in the importance and practice of listening to the "God whispers" or the Universe and living in gratitude.

There are many ways to hone the practice of "listening" for guidance, and one way that I've used for years is walking. I feel energized and renewed by nature, especially when I'm near water, but I also love hiking paths surrounded by trees, rivers, and the chance encounter with animals. The natural environment inspires me, and I can remember several times in my life that I have gasped at the beauty I'm exposed to by taking the time to look. I say this because if you're like me, you've had times that your mind is so overwhelmed with thoughts, your heart overfilled with emotions, and your spirit overburdened by a dull ache that you don't take the time to actually "see" what's in front of you. The beauty around you goes unnoticed in these moments.

The famous painter Georgia O'Keeffe once said, "When you take a flower in your hand and really look at it, it's your world for the moment. I want to give that world to someone else. Most people in the city rush around so, they have no time to look at a flower. I want them to see it whether they want to or not."

It's important to be present and aware or we miss the extraordinary moments in our lives.

I'm realistic and know that sometimes the circumstances of life cause overwhelm; I've been there on more than one occasion! I've seen the dangers of not spending any time in my metaphorical rooms (physical, mental, emotional, and spiritual) to spending too much time in one room at the expense of another. As the Indian Proverb, *A House With Four Rooms* states, " Most of us tend to live in one room most of the time, but unless we go into every room every day, even if only to keep it aired, we are not a complete person."

There are times I am stuck in my "head" and need to stop the constant grinding of the wheels. It is exhausting trying to keep up with the thoughts and ideas; this constant grinding litters the other areas of my life. Time management becomes crucial in scheduling important appointments, exercise time, and leisure activities.

A major problem for me is insomnia. Can you imagine trying to stay focused and effective in carrying out everyday duties without a good night's sleep? I've had to learn important self-care strategies to help me in order to stay healthy. Staying healthy has become even more important to me after experiencing a serious health crisis that led to open-heart surgery. Some of us need a "wake up" call, and this was mine.

Coping with grief is another fact of life that we all deal with and for some of us, our days seem to be layered in grief. Our emotions pull and stretch us to our limits like a rubber band; when our emotions are pulled and stretched, our tempers can flare and tears can stream down our faces uncontrollably. There can be any number of stressful situations that layer our lives: deaths, divorce, addictions, and loss (relationships, employment, etc.). Being pulled and stretched in different directions isn't a place to dwell; not only for health reasons, but it weakens the foundation of your life. One must take action to "air" out the emotional room to stay connected and in balance with life.

In what ways do you describe an ordinary day? If your day is anything like mine, you may eat on the run or overindulge in delicious horderves, meals, desserts, and snacks. Stepping on the scale or looking closely in the mirror or at a photograph may be evidence that this lifestyle isn't providing the desired results one wants. For some people, we climb on the hamster wheel, not for exercise but for the development and continuation of some of our bad habits: overeating, watching too much television, or staying plugged into the internet for hours. In times of chaos, diet and exercise can be the first thing crossed off our daily calendar, not because it got done, but because we fill that time slot with other activities. It seems to be one of the first things we shove aside, and as that hamster wheel goes round, we feel bad and guilt wells up. I've been there.

I can remember when I was a kid a church bus picked me up early on Sunday mornings for Sunday School. The community was terrific, and I enjoyed the fellowship and music. Going to church was also a way to escape the house for a while. Over the years I have visited several churches and explored different religious doctrines. At one point, early on in my spiritual exploration, I had an experience that had me bargaining with God. This bargain led me to study New Thought communities, and as a practitioner, I have developed a life based on principles that provide guidance in my life and have provided my vision for extraordinary moments.

In order to create a "complete" life as described in the Indian Proverb, it's essential that steps be taken to "air" out the four rooms every single day. There are a plethora of ways to do this, and one chooses what methods and how much time is needed in each room.

I believe it is important for our self-care to follow routines. For example, I like to walk first thing in the morning. If I don't take my walk in the morning, it may not get rescheduled into my daily activities.

The planner I use helps me organize my daily activities and record specific items that are included in my action plan. For me, routines and organization help me "air" out my rooms. This doesn't mean that I don't get entangled and thrown off my path from time to time because I do. When this happens, I recognize the detour and get right back on my path. It's similar to when I'm on a diet and I partake in something that isn't on my diet. I don't tell myself that I blew it so I can eat whatever for the rest of the day...I pivot and get back on my plan toward extraordinary moments.

It took quite a bit of time for me to learn the pivot process, but when I did, my life changed for the better. Because I think we are all teachers and learners at the same time, I continue to learn and practice the pivot. I've established other self-care practices and have rituals that help me keep my balance with a busy life, and I'm having a blast because even the ordinary is extraordinary.

A House With Four Rooms (physical, mental, emotional, and spiritual) advocates a balanced lifestyle plan for all practitioners, and the practice allows us to live a "complete" life. A life that recognizes that we can learn from everything and know that the ordinary can certainly be extraordinary!

CHAPTER 2

EXTRAORDINARY MOMENTS JOURNAL
ACTIVITY

*E*arly in my adulthood, I learned from reading author Rumer Godden the Indian Proverb or axiom that says "Everyone should think of themselves as a house with four rooms: physical, mental, an emotional, and a spiritual. Most of us tend to live in one room most of the time, but unless we go into every room every day, even if only to keep it aired, we are not a complete person."

As an Achievement Coach, I've referred back to this proverb often, whether to remind myself or share its wisdom with thousands of others that desire to live an *Intentional Life*.

EXERCISE from: Extraordinary Moments

1. Describe your ordinary day.

_____

_____

_____

_____

_____

2. Make a list of your self-care practices.

-
-
-
-
-
-
-
-
-

3. What routines do you have in your life?

_____

_____

_____

_____

_____

_____

_____

_____

_____

_____

~

CHAPTER 3

MAPPING OUT YOUR INTENTIONAL LIFE

The excitement of the birth of my latest granddaughter found me smiling from ear to ear. On a recent visit with my son, daughter-in-law, and grandson, we talked about the birth of their daughter and the upcoming birthday celebration for my grandson. My son's family is multicultural; my Korean daughter-in-law teaches my grandchildren about their Korean culture through language, traditions, and food. This exposure to the world will shape their perspective on everything from relationships, self-esteem, and self-confidence to ultimately making decisions and forming their opinions about life.

The people, places, and events in one's life, particularly in early childhood, are the foundation of teaching and learning that create core beliefs and fundamentally define who we are and how we see ourselves. My grandchildren are fortunate to have this positive foundation in their lives.

The way we see ourselves is connected to our core beliefs. When I examine belief systems, I look for patterns and make connections. Some beliefs that seem ingrained in us were developed from those early stages of life; we learned from the people and events that we were born into, and each situation had lessons to teach us. Unfortunately, some of us are not as fortunate as my grandchildren. For example, my early years were spent in an environment that harbored ill feelings brought on by verbal and physical abuse. I was often told that I wasn't "good enough" or "capable," and the folks questioned whether I'd even graduate from high school. I decided early on that their words and speculation were not really mine to carry; I chose to work hard toward my goals to prove to them and myself that I could achieve what I put effort into. It was at this time that my *Pilgrimage to Self* began.

I defined myself as a wife, mother, teacher, and friend for many years. In the busyness of life, I had forgotten and lost myself. Once I returned to my *Pilgrimage to Self*, I set out to discover "Who am I?" There are many ways to identify and connect to *who I am and who I want to be*. For starters, from the lessons and experiences I have had, I developed boundaries around my path in life. These boundaries have not been set to contain me and stunt my intellectual, spiritual, physical, and mental growth, but they have been structured by fence posts carved with respect for myself and others; they have been connected by faith, love, and desire.

It is essential to reflect on your core beliefs and, if needed, reframe experiences and early learning to develop new beliefs that serve your life's purpose. My journey is proof that paradigm shifts do exist and that we do indeed have the power to build the life we are meant to lead.

So my journey began with the realization that I am not defined by the words "not good enough," whether supplied by myself or others. My journey continues with the acceptance that I am not perfect, but I can strive for excellence in whatever areas of my life I choose. This realization was made after many hard knocks, stumbling, and an honest intention to prevail and succeed.

On my journey, I've also learned that I'm not in competition with anyone else; I shouldn't compare myself to anyone else because my journey is my own. There can be many obstacles to overcome to get to and stay on the path, but I don't have to be one of those obstacles. I also don't have to invite obstacles onto my path, so I choose not to participate in gossip or with people that are quick to tear others down; it can be challenging when people ask inappropriate questions or make judgmental comments with little or no genuine concern or feelings for you. We've all been there...when so-called friends and family are busy sharing their personal thoughts and feelings about your private business with everyone and their brother.

These experiences taught me that boundaries must be created to learn and grow into a better version of myself each day. So, rather than compare myself to others, I learn from them. When it comes to boundaries, I recognize that I'm not limited by others, the wrongful beliefs of others, or by the old faulty beliefs I developed about myself, the world, or my God from my early learning. I am free to create and live the extraordinary life I desire by practicing and living in the Truth. I am responsible for creating my world, and with this knowledge, I have developed personal Maps to enrich my life. I rely on my Maps to guide me, and when I need assistance in finding my way, I can refer to them and the paths I've chosen.

The Maps I have developed coordinate with my *four rooms.* My Intellectual Map has paths that lead me to learn new things and expand my scope of knowledge. My Emotional Map allows me to rely on paths I've identified that help me cope and will enable me to experience peace and serenity. My Physical Map is filled with paths and trails that provide wellness opportunities, and my Spirituality Map guides me with paths of prayer, meditation, spiritual readings, and practices. My personal Maps influence the direction I choose to go each day, and if I get off track, I go right back to my Maps for guidance.

I remain open to learning and growing, creating the extraordinary I desire in everything I do and experience. I've heard people say that a rebirth of sorts happens when faced with a health crisis, and I know this too is true of my own health crisis. After complications from multiple pulmonary emboli, open-heart surgery, and a blood disorder, I'm living my second chance. This second chance has renewed my faith in my daily practices, my personal planner, and my Mapping system to help me "air" out my *four rooms* and create a balanced life filled with extraordinary experiences and people.

If you are interested in creating your own personal planner and Maps, continue to do the exercises in the journal activities. But for now, know there are many ways to identify the paths that are right for you: begin by identifying what you want in your life, what brings you joy, what makes your heart sing, and what your extraordinary looks like. Once you have these ideas, you've identified areas to focus on for constructing your paths and creating your Maps.

While I have you thinking, how about answering a few more questions? How would you define who you are? What are some of your core beliefs? How were these beliefs developed? It is essential to reflect on this because your learning experiences influence your beliefs, and if your core beliefs do not serve you, it is time for a paradigm shift.

Now give some thought to these questions. What boundaries have you established? What expectations do you have for how you treat people or how they treat you? What boundaries would you like to establish for your relationships with others? How about the relationship with yourself?

Another piece of this puzzle in developing personal Maps is understanding where you spend your time. You must invest your time on the paths that serve you and lead you to your heart's desire. This is the self-care part of the journey, and this all takes time and a commitment.

CHAPTER 4

MAPPING OUT YOUR INTENTIONAL LIFE
JOURNAL ACTIVITY

*E*xercise from: Mapping Out Your Intentional Life

1. What brings you joy?

_____

_____

_____

_____

_____

_____

_____

_____

_____

2. How would you define who you are?

----

3. What are some of your core beliefs?

_____

_____

_____

_____

_____

_____

_____

_____

_____

_____

_____

_____

_____

_____

_____

_____

_____

_____

_____

_____

LISA MCGRATH

4. How were these beliefs developed?

----

5. What boundaries have you established in your life?

_____

_____

_____

_____

_____

_____

_____

_____

_____

_____

_____

_____

_____

_____

_____

_____

_____

_____

_____

6. What expectations do you have for the way you treat people or how they treat you?

_____

_____

_____

_____

_____

_____

_____

_____

_____

_____

_____

_____

_____

_____

_____

_____

_____

_____

7. What boundaries would you like to establish for all your relationships with others?

----

8. What boundaries would you like to establish for yourself?

----

9. Where and on what activities do you spend the bulk of your time?

-
-
-
-
-
-
-
-
-
-
-
-
-
-
-
-
-
-
-
-

10. Where and on what activities would you like to develop in your life?

∾

CHAPTER 5

WHAT DOES IT MEAN TO LIVE WITH PURPOSE?

I've been thinking about the idea of living with purpose for quite some time; I've researched, read, and written about living an *Intentional Life*. It's an interesting concept and something that can have a positive impact on your entire life. When we live with purpose, we get more done, we create meaning in our lives, and most importantly, we feel happier and more fulfilled. That's why it's an important topic to discuss. It's also what inspired me to create my coaching programs and write this book.

Over the course of this book, we'll take a look at living with purpose and how we can start to live more intentionally. We'll look at how this will affect all aspects of our lives and of course, I will have plenty of hands-on tips and suggestions for you.

Let's start straight away by talking a little bit about what it means to live with purpose. In essence, it means that you know what you're doing. You have goals and are passionate about what you do. Instead of simply letting the days pass you by, you work with purpose to make the most from each day and move closer to making your dreams and goals a reality.

Living with a purpose has a couple of big advantages over simply existing. When you know exactly what you want to do with your life, you have a clear plan or path. You don't have to dread getting up each morning and then try to figure out what you will do. Your plan becomes a way to eliminate *decision fatigue* because you've made a lot of your daily decisions already and can concentrate on what you need to do. You simply jump in and keep working towards the goals you set based on your purpose and the direction you've chosen.

When you live an *Intentional Life,* you have a clear set of *core values* that you follow, based on your purpose. This will come in handy anytime you have a decision to make. Think of these values as your compass that keeps you on track and allows you to stay on the PATHS of Purpose.

Most importantly though, living with purpose gives you a great sense of self-worth. You know what you're doing and you're actively working towards the goals you've set yourself. Not only does this increase your feeling of self-worth and self-confidence, living a purpose-driven and fulfilled life will also greatly increase your overall happiness.

Happiness is an *inside* job, so when you feel more confident, see progress towards your goals, and live with purpose, it is natural to feel happier.

Making the decision to be *happy* is a great start. For some, this is a difficult idea and seems too rudimentary, but it is essential to creating your best life. It is much easier to build on a solid foundation, and when you establish healthy routines that support your physical, mental, emotional, and spiritual wellbeing, you create that solid foundation.

In the end, that's what it's really about, isn't it? We all want to live a happy and fulfilled life with meaning. That's why it's important to start thinking about living with purpose...living an *Intentional Life.*

Make sure to complete the exercise prompts in the journal activity chapters to create a guiding Map to your *Intentional Life*.

FINDING MY PURPOSE

"We all want to live a happy and fulfilled life with meaning. That's why it's important to start thinking about living with purpose...living an *Intentional Life*." ~ Lisa McGrath

My pilgrimages across Spain along the Camino de Santiago empowered me to share my journey and pursue my dreams.

CHAPTER 6

WHAT DOES IT MEAN TO LIVE WITH PURPOSE? JOURNAL ACTIVITY

*E*xercise from: What Does It Mean To Live With Purpose?

1. What does happiness feel like for you?

_____

_____

_____

_____

_____

_____

_____

_____

_____

2. Make a list of the common decisions you make each day.

-
-
-
-
-
-
-
-
-
-
-
-
-
-
-
-
-
-
-
-

3. To avoid *decision fatigue,* which decisions could you make in advance? (*what to eat for breakfast and lunch, what outfit to wear each day, where to park, etc.*)

-
-
-
-
-
-
-
-
-
-
-
-
-
-
-
-
-
-

~

CHAPTER 7

WHY IT'S IMPORTANT TO FIND YOUR PURPOSE

I want to dive a little deeper and talk more about why it is important to find your purpose. Making the decision to live your life with purpose, and then finding said purpose can have a profound effect on your life. It has a way of defining who you are and what you do. It gives your life meaning.

When you decide on your life's purpose, it gives what you do a lot more meaning. Every step along the way and all the work you do towards reaching your goals serves to bring you one step closer, and it becomes much easier to get things done when they are done with purpose and with a firm goal in mind. You'll feel more energized and excited about each new day. Image waking up feeling refreshed and excited about your day.

Living with purpose also helps you define and set a system of core values that will guide you throughout the coming years. For some of us, we adopted the values and belief systems of others; the things we use to measure our own progress are based on someone else's standards. You'll find reevaluating your belief systems and developing your own value system beneficial in all areas of your life. When you do have your own systems, you don't have to waste time and energy each day trying to figure out if what you're doing is right or worth doing. As long as it aligns with your purpose, you know you're on the right track. That gives you a lot of confidence in what you are doing.

When you are living with purpose and working towards a worthwhile goal, you take a lot of pride in what you do. Your energy increases, and with each passing day and each small step that you move forward towards that goal, your sense of self-worth also increases. Having this momentum allows you to use that feeling to propel you through the next day and any of the next challenges on your PATH.

Living a life with purpose, that's meaningful and gives you a sense of self-worth and confidence, leads to experiencing much more happiness in your life.

Create a purpose for yourself that aligns with your values, provides meaning, and excites you. The true secret to a happy life is being completely fulfilled by the life you're living...by living an *Intentional Life*.

We are social creatures who need to make a difference and have a purpose, and for most of us, we want to find a place in society where we fit in and create impact. We may think that material things bring us happiness, but what truly matters is how meaningful, helpful, and purposeful what we do is. And when you live an *Intentional Life*, with each new day, don't be surprised to notice a measurable increase in your overall happiness on this journey towards a purpose-driven life.

One of the most beneficial practices you can adopt for yourself is keeping a journal. Use your journal to make note of your thoughts, ideas, and do the exercises suggested for "airing out" your four rooms. Many of the exercises you'll find yourself returning to over and over again because they make a difference in your life.

Last but not least, living with purpose is good for your health. Being needed, being helpful, and adding value to the lives of others have a measurable effect on your physical, mental, emotional, and spiritual health.

Living a purposeful life decreases your risk of heart disease and stroke, while it is also protecting you against depression. In fact, one of the best ways to fight depression is to find meaning and purpose in what you do each and every day.

A House With Four Rooms suggests doing something daily in each of your four rooms: physical, mental, emotional, and spiritual. In this way, you will move forward towards your desired results...complete well-being, experiencing the ordinary as extraordinary, and living an *Intentional Life* of meaning and purpose.

It is an essential self-care strategy to not only discover your purpose but to live it...in every area of your life. Take some time for yourself today and begin thinking about your values systems...it's time to start discovering and defining your personal value system.

CHAPTER 8

WHY IT'S IMPORTANT TO FIND YOUR PURPOSE JOURNAL ACTIVITY

*E*xercise from: Why It's Important To Find Your Purpose

When answering these questions, think about examples in your social life, career, finances, and even in your closest relationships.

1. Who are the people in your life that you have the closest relationships?

-
-
-
-
-
-
-
-

2. How would you define each relationship?

_____

_____

_____

_____

_____

_____

_____

_____

_____

_____

_____

_____

_____

_____

_____

_____

_____

_____

3. What are your most prominent characteristics?

----

4. What are your finest personal qualities?

_____

_____

_____

_____

_____

_____

_____

_____

_____

_____

_____

_____

_____

_____

_____

_____

_____

_____

5. How would you NOT like to be remembered?

----

6. What have been your proudest moments in your life?

_____

_____

_____

_____

_____

_____

_____

_____

_____

_____

_____

_____

_____

_____

_____

_____

_____

∼

CHAPTER 9

FINDING A PURPOSE & SETTING GOALS

*N*othing much can get in between someone who is championing a cause...ask me how I know...I go "all in" and passion takes over. Whether personal or global, having a purpose and setting goals to achieve it is a powerful thing. The drive it takes to power through and achieve the outcome builds unshakable confidence along the way.

The confidence you experience in one situation is the same confidence you carry into other situations where you might not have had enough experience in yet to predict the outcomes.

When working on goals with purpose, it creates stamina, determination, perseverance, and grit.

These are game-changing qualities that shift mindsets and abilities from average to extraordinary. This is a major confidence builder. People who have developed these sorts of skills are not wallflowers. Their grit and determination level them up to a new playing field and they are willing to pivot, believe in second chances, and keep pursuing their dreams even when they reach a point that most people would quit.

Sometimes you want change so badly, you set goals that require you to dig deep and do hard things to accomplish the quest. Your purpose may be weight loss, getting a degree, opening a business, or improving your credit score. These goals may seem out of reach, but with the right mindset and hard work, they are achievable. As my mentor, Stu McLaren, says, "We're better together."

From a work situation that must be completed to a health scare that requires you to focus and set goals, sometimes you aren't looking to be the person who can do these things, but you have no choice. These goals may seem unfair and punitive, but like any other goal, they are achievable and once you do, you won't believe the confidence they produce. And I want you to know that YOU do not have to go on this journey of change alone...find a mentor, coach, or group to help you overcome limiting mindset, imposter syndrome, or the countless other issues that tend to pop up when one is trying to sift through antiquated belief systems, developing personal values, and discovering purpose for a more meaningful life.

Sometimes the outcomes are incredibly motivating and enticing; they provide the momentum to help you pivot and start on the goal and adventure. From a new body emerging from lifting weights to learning to walk with a prosthesis, you can be highly motivated to get in there and succeed. If you are thrilled to be chasing the goal, get in there and do what must be done, and take the prize.

As an Achievement Coach, I'm not just a cheerleader because I ask you the hard questions, push you forward, and become your accountability partner...I want YOU to succeed! I've witnessed the transformation that is possible by helping hundreds of people discover their purpose, align their values, set boundaries, design their lives, and develop the action steps to get them moving forward toward their goals.

For some, failure can lead to something big. A huge loss - or worse, not making the goal - can have worse consequences than you'd like so you are called to work harder to ensure you don't fail. It is important to use that fear to motivate you and watch the motivation turn into confidence; confidence then becomes a driving force to get you where you want to be.

This is true in the case of my client, Brenda, who spent lots of time, money, and energy pursuing the wrong dream...her mother's dream for her. She was the first generation to finish high school and attend college. Over the years, her mother groomed her and prepared her for the "something better" that she herself hadn't achieved. She wanted Brenda to have a career that would provide the income to support herself and make a better life for her, so Brenda pursued an education in nursing. She hated every minute of it, started missing classes, failing classes, and giving up on the dream. It was easier for her to give up on the dream of becoming a nurse because it wasn't her dream...it was her mother's dream. Brenda found hope in a pivot when she changed her focus and zeroed in on a physical therapy program to earn her doctorate. With the pivot to follow her own dreams, she gained confidence, momentum, and success in the program and within herself.

Sometimes you may feel like you want to give up, in a word: **DON'T.** Just put your focus on the goal, design a plan of action, and do the work. Do it. Feel it. Work it. Earn it. And know that YOU do NOT have to go on this journey alone!

Setting goals and working towards a purpose takes a lot of energy and determination and working through the obstacles builds the grit and grace needed to persevere and dig deep. It also helps you develop the confidence in yourself to achieve those big dreams, to accomplish your goals, and to live your *Intentional Life*.

But where do you start?

Goals are merely the desires we have that are made precise with a deadline attached to them. To feel like you're, genuinely moving forward and making adequate progress in life, it's crucial that the goals you commit to pursuing each play a part in driving you forwards toward accomplishing a far greater vision.

Setting and achieving healthy goals is essential to health and happiness. This is important for your physical, mental, emotional, and spiritual wellbeing. Striving towards healthy goals expresses that you're the boss of your life and that life isn't the boss of you. Having goals is always a good thing for complete wellbeing.

Visualizing a goal is much more important than having all the answers about how it's going to actualize. The first stage in the construction of a house is the creation of a set of plans that show the end vision of what the house will eventually look like. Without this set of plans, it will be impossible for those involved in building the house to know what the end product should look like. If you don't have a clear vision of what you want to accomplish in life, you can end up spending years, going around in circles, committing to things that you don't care about, and frustrated with the world in general. People who aren't actively working towards a goal or a vision in life will often experience life as being meaningless and directionless.

The great news is that life doesn't have to be this way!

Although many people assume that getting a vision for their future will be a challenging and time-consuming process, it isn't.

A meaningful vision for your future can be as simple as making a difference in the life of one other person, or, it could be impacting the world on an enormous geographical scale - and everything in-between! The first step of goal setting is to define your vision, and take full responsibility for what it is that you want to achieve. This vision cannot be what you think other people want you to do, or even what you 'think' is just a good idea.

It's important to understand that 'good' ideas do not come from the same place as meaningful visions. Ideas come from our heads, and visions come from our hearts.

The vision and goals that you develop for your future can not be what other people want or expect from you because the purpose here is not to please others, but to find something that will motivate you for the rest of your life (or, for the next couple of years at least).

If you don't have a vision for your future, consider the best-case scenario about what you could achieve in your life in five years from now. Doing this should give you a starting point for defining one or two goals (at least).

If you want to succeed with goal setting, you need to define your most important goals throughout your full range of life areas. Without having a set of targets in life that inspire you, you won't have much clarity of focus and direction for your future.

Goal setting allows you to take control of your life's direction and also provides you with a benchmark that can be used to determine whether you're making progress towards these goals, or whether you're not.

Firstly, though, to accomplish any goals in life, you need to know how to set goals because goal setting is a process that starts with careful consideration of what you genuinely want to achieve. The part of the goal-setting process that most people don't like is often the (guaranteed) hard work that'll be required to accomplish them!

In between setting goals and achieving them is a series of five steps that transcend the specifications of each goal. Understanding these steps will allow you to set realistic goals that you can confidently accomplish.

Tip: Only Set Goals that Inspire You

When you set goals for yourself, it's crucial that they inspire you, that they are important to you, and that achieving them will positively benefit the world in some way. If your goals are small, irrelevant to anyone's quality of life, or uninspiring, then the chances of you investing time into making them happen is slim. Genuine inspiration is the key principle behind successful goal setting. It's important to set goals that are in alignment with your top priorities in life because if you don't have this degree of focus, you stand at risk of feeling overwhelmed by them and giving up too soon due to not even knowing where to start tackling them.

Tip: Schedule the daily activities you must do to achieve your goals.

Goal achievement requires commitment, patience, persistence, and perseverance - and with any of these elements missing from the goal-setting equation, your chances of fulfilling these goals are limited. So to maximize your chances of goal-setting success, remember to make sure that your goals are both inspiring and relevant to you.

Having a solid foundation in your four rooms allows you to pursue additional personal and professional goals in each area of your life that aligns with your values and purpose.

Much of this discovery process begins with self-awareness and reflection so you can zero in on what excites you, brings you joy, and satisfies your definition of success.

For your personal and professional development, create goals in all significant areas of your life. Some of the categories that I work with for my master goal-setting come from defining my priority life areas:

• Social & Family Relationships

• Career & Educational Aspirations

• Money & Personal Finances

• Recreation & Leisure

• Life's Routine Responsibilities

• Giving Back to Society & Contribution

• Physical, Mental, Emotional, and Spiritual Health

Self-Awareness must be your focus; it comes from visiting your mental and emotional rooms, observing your thoughts, and tracking your actions. It helps develop your commitment, willpower, and perseverance to move forward with taking action towards your goals. The feeling that comes from doing whatever it takes is a wonderful building block for self-esteem and confidence; it is a way to learn *who* you are and *what* is important to you as a person.

∾

CREATING A VISION

Each year I create a Self-Portrait Vision Board as a visual aid for my manifesting practice. As I do my visualization exercises throughout the year, I'm amazed by the accuracy of my picture and word portrayals.

You do not have to wait until the start of a new year to create your Self-Portrait Vision Board.

Start clipping magazine pictures and words that resonate with the *Intentional Life* you want to experience.

Don't stop at magazines; use your own photographs, find images online, or create your own.

Make sure to select photographs that represent the emotions and characteristics you desire, the experiences you'd like to have, and the places you want to go. Your Vision Board should reflect YOU, not just the material items you wish to own.

~

CHAPTER 10

FINDING A PURPOSE & SETTING GOALS
JOURNAL ACTIVITY

*E*xercise from: Finding a Purpose & Setting Goals

1. Define what 'success' genuinely means to you.

_____

_____

_____

_____

_____

_____

_____

_____

_____

_____
_____
_____
_____
_____
_____
_____
_____
_____
_____
_____
_____
_____
_____
_____
_____
_____
_____
_____
_____

2. What are your main life areas?

-
-
-
-
-
-
-
-

3. What is the purpose of life?

----

4. What is your greatest life vision?

_____

_____

_____

_____

_____

_____

_____

_____

_____

_____

_____

_____

_____

_____

_____

_____

_____

_____

_____

5. What value do you contribute to the world and all of the other people who are in it?

----

6. Life is all about balance, and it's only you who knows the right balance for you. Although it can be hard to articulate our greatest life vision, attempt to visualize what your life would be like if it were perfect in every way. Imagine if all the people you know were to know exactly how kind, loving, caring, and giving you could be. How would you like all these people to remember you?

CHAPTER 11

6 SECRETS TO LIVING ON PURPOSE AND ACHIEVING YOUR GOALS

*W*hy do you suppose that so many people never achieve their goals in life? The answer, unfortunately, is that they never set them. It's so true -- to the extent that only one in five Americans reach the age of 67 without having to depend on Social Security, and that includes people in supposedly high-paying professions like doctors and lawyers.

Most people don't plan for the future at all. They work during the week and spend what they earned on the weekends. They waste their money, time, and energy.

Studies show that most people...about 80%...that make New Year's Resolutions have given up by mid-February. Of course, we don't have to wait for a new year or new month to start making progress on our goals...we can start right now with a commitment to ourselves.

So, if about 80% of people are quitting on themselves and their goals, what are you to do? We know giving up is a great waste of a powerful, natural resource: the human mind. With a bit of mindset work, you have the opportunity to change that...it takes a commitment to yourself and a promise to visit your metaphorical rooms as described by the philosophy of *A House With Four Rooms*.

Did you know that once we set a target or goal, our mind becomes an automatic system that monitors feedback regarding that target? According to Dr. Maxwell Maltz in *Psycho-Cybernetics*, once you set a goal, your mind adjusts your course depending on any new data it gets. One of Dr. Maltz's points is that it begins with the "mental portrait" or self-image we create for ourselves from all of our experiences, successes, and failures, and feelings and behaviors.

When you make your goals, your brain makes corrections so that you can stay on target. The more specific the goal is, the better the corrections are. Furthermore, our brains work with our imaginations and can't distinguish between an event that really took place and one that was vividly imagined. So, if you clearly and firmly set a goal, for your brain it is as if the goal has already been achieved.

Take the time now to write a goal statement. Write it in the first person, using pronouns like "I," "my," "mine," and "me." Keep your goal statements short and to the point. Be emphatic. Be positive. For instance, "I am raising my self-esteem with positive statements and positive actions today."

Remember, the more specific you make your goals, the better your chance to achieve them. These techniques may be helpful to you:

1. Set short-range goals that will build toward your long-range goals. Start with short time periods, such as a week or a month, and then build your long-term goals for six months, one year, or five years. When you use a specific timeframe, it helps you measure your success.

2. Set goals that inspire you, but that are also realistic and achievable. Set a series of goals so that you are going step-by-step. That way, it is easier to adjust them as needed. Along the way. It also inspires confidence in you as you keep reaching your goals.

3. Share your goals with an individual or group who might have similar goals. It's great reinforcement.

4. Celebrate the achievement of your goals with rewards. It could be a small reward at each step along the way or a bigger reward like a trip or a dinner when you've achieved milestones.

5. Keep your goals somewhere where you can access them easily. Don't write them and put them away somewhere since out of sight usually means out of mind.

6. Guard your goals. Don't share them with negative people who probably won't encourage you. Share them with positive people who wish you well.

 Now that you know what a powerful tool goal setting is, why don't you start making use of it today?

It's a powerful but easy way to help you achieve the success you want because the brain is very powerful and has the ability to adapt and change with repeated exposure, practice, and attention. You can use daily exercises to improve memory, increase focus, processing speeds, problem-solving skills, and just to feel healthier.

CHAPTER 12

6 SECRETS TO LIVING ON PURPOSE AND ACHIEVING YOUR GOALS JOURNAL ACTIVITY

*E*xercises from: 6 Secrets to Living on Purpose and Achieving Your Goals

1. Set short-range goals that will build toward your long-range goals. Start with short time periods, such as a week or a month, and then build your long-term goals for six months, one year, or five years. When you use a specific timeframe, it helps you measure your success. Use this prompt template to describe your long-range goals and the short-range goals needed to achieve success. Remember to include a realistic timeframe that breaks the long-range goal into smaller increments.

• Describe a Long-Range Goal:

- Long-Range Time Frame:

_____

_____

_____

_____

- Short-Range Goal 1 that supports Long-Range Goal 1:

_____

_____

- Time Frame:

_____

_____

- Short-Range Goal 2 that supports Long-Range Goal 1:

_____

_____

- Time Frame:

_____

_____

- Short-Range Goal 3 that supports Long-Range Goal 1:

_____

_____

- Time Frame:

_____

_____

• Short-Range Goal 4 that supports Long-Range Goal 1:

_____

_____

• Time Frame:

_____

_____

• Short-Range Goal 5 that supports Long-Range Goal 1:

_____

_____

• Time Frame:

_____

_____

2. Set goals that inspire you, but that are also realistic and achievable. Set a series of goals so that you are going step-by-step. That way, it is easier to adjust them as needed. Along the way. It also inspires confidence in you as you keep reaching your goals. What are some goals you'd like to work toward?

•

•

•

•

•

•

•

•

-
-
-
-
-
-
-
-
-
-

3. Share your goals with an individual or group who might have similar goals. It's great reinforcement. Who will you share your goals and invite to be your accountability partner?

-
-
-

4. Celebrate the achievement of your goals with rewards. It could be a small reward at each step along the way or a bigger reward like a trip or a dinner when you've achieved milestones. Make a list of achievement rewards.

-
-
-
-
-

-
-
-
-
-
-
-
-
-

5. Keep your goals somewhere where you can access them easily. Don't write them and put them away somewhere since out of sight usually means out of mind. Tape a copy to your bathroom mirror, refrigerator, and computer screen. Write a list of positive affirmations to include with your list of goals.

-
-
-
-
-
-
-
-
-
-

6. Guard your goals. Don't share them with negative people who probably won't encourage you. Share them with positive people who wish you well.

-

-

-

~

CHAPTER 13

GETTING CLEAR ABOUT YOUR PURPOSE AND BELIEFS BOOSTS CONFIDENCE

*H*aving a strong sense of self is imperative to loving yourself and to living an *Intentional Life*. Self-awareness helps you to better understand yourself and what drives your behavior. This understanding helps you to be more compassionate with yourself when times are tough. Similarly, having a strong sense of purpose can help to solidify your self-love. When you know what you want to do with your life, it's easier to recognize your own value and to feel more love for yourself. Getting clear about your purpose can help boost your confidence, and it gets you on the PATHS to living your *Intentional Life*.

Purpose can have a wide array of definitions. For this step, consider your purpose to be your "why." For example, why do you do what you do? What is the underlying motivation you have for working, playing, relating to others, etc.? If you don't know the answer to this, it's time to start giving it some thought. Take notes on these questions and look for patterns of what drives you. Knowing your strongest motivation or purpose in life is important to a number of things, including your success, happiness, and self-confidence.

When you practice visiting your four rooms each day, you'll soon discover patterns that develop. For example, for your physical room, you may notice you enjoy a particular exercise routine, riding a bike, walking, or participating in a team sport. Choose fun activities.

Notice how you feel when you "air" out each room and do more of what you enjoy. My mental room includes several different routines that enrich my life and bring me joy: daily reading, journaling, writing, and learning new things. A visit to your mental room can consist of thoughtful reflection, great conversations, and exploring and learning about new places, people, and things.

In the emotional room, it is essential to develop coping skills that you can rely on when faced with uncertainty or troubling circumstances. For me, my practice includes breathing exercises that allow me to pause, remain calm, and decide how I want to respond at any given moment.

There are many ways to "air" your spiritual room; for me, daily prayer and meditation practices are regular routines that guide me throughout my day. Reading spiritual texts has been important to my daily spiritual wellbeing.

When you understand what's most important to you in life, you can then take proactive actions based on those priorities. This is the secret sauce to living an *Intentional Life*. Living in accordance with your purpose will lead you to feel better about yourself because you know you're making decisions that are in line with your values and that you're making strides toward doing the things that will help you to reach your goals.

When you have purpose in your life, you have taken steps to declare what's important to you and what matters most. This mapping is an important step in the process. This can be quite empowering, and it can also lead to increased self-esteem when you're living on your own terms, not ones determined by outside forces.

Developing your sense of purpose and discovering just what that is can be the tricky part. Fortunately, there are some things you can do to move that process along. Taking stock of what matters most to you and your priorities in life is a good start. Taking action on becoming more self-aware is an essential practice. As noted earlier, you can make a list of these things and look for patterns to guide your next steps. It's also helpful to get out there and try new things. The more experiences and people you expose yourself to, the more likely you are to find something that speaks to you, aligns with your values, and influences your future decisions.

If you're not sure what you want to try, start with things that interest you or that you've considered trying in the past, then go from there. Keep in mind that you don't have to settle for just one purpose. There could be multiple things that sustain your interest and push you forward each and every day.

This is just a short summary of what purpose is and how it contributes to confidence and your *Intentional Life*. It's time to start seeking your own life's purpose. Soon, you'll find yourself living a life you love. When you get clear on your purpose, your confidence, self-esteem, and energy all increase...it's such a great boost!

～

CHAPTER 14

GETTING CLEAR ABOUT YOUR PURPOSE AND BELIEFS BOOSTS CONFIDENCE JOURNAL ACTIVITY

*E*xercise from: Getting Clear About Your Purpose and Beliefs Boosts Confidence

It's important to decide what the important areas in our lives are. It's critical that we maintain this perspective as we commit to improving one area in our life, without turning our back on all of the other areas. The philosophy of *A House With Four Rooms* is to visit each of the major four rooms (physical, mental, emotional, and spiritual) daily; remember, you don't have to spend great lengths of time in each, but you must go in each to "air" it out.

1. What impact is pursuing these goals likely to have on my time?

----

2. What else could suffer the consequences of my divided attention if I commit to this pursuit?

----

3. In what ways does this effort compliment (or detract from) my greatest life vision? Although this may sound a little sadistic, this line of self-inquiry can be hugely clarifying. Because if we don't commit to pursuing our greatest life vision, we might end up compromising our standards on a daily basis.

∾

CHAPTER 15

ARE YOU BEING INTENTIONAL WITH YOUR TIME? A TIME LOG CAN HELP

*H*ave you ever tracked how much time you spend on your various activities throughout the day? If you haven't, it may be an eye-opening exercise for you...especially as we begin the process of "airing out" our physical, mental, emotional, and spiritual rooms.

From my own experience, I have to remind myself of the health risks of sitting too much as it's the new smoking crisis. Being self-aware and taking control of my time is essential to living my *Intentional Life* and keeping healthy.

Try it out for a couple of days, or a week if you dare. It may seem tedious at first, but it will pay off in the end. Diligently tracking what you spend your time on will help you be much more productive going forward. It will help you prioritize your to-do list, align your commitments with your purpose, and zero in on your goals.

A time log, or activity log, is essentially a log of how much time you spend on each activity you do during a set time period. It can be written manually in a notebook, tracked electronically on an app on a mobile device, or entered into a spreadsheet on a computer.

The important thing is to remember to write down every single thing you do during the day and how much time you spend doing it. Other categories you may want to track could include if the activity was planned, if you were supposed to do it at a different time (earlier or later or even a different day), the value or importance of the activity, how you feel (emotions and energy level), and any miscellaneous notes.

Tracking how much time you spend on each activity throughout the day will make it easy to look at the full picture of your schedule. It will show you how you spend your time, what time of day you are most productive, how you feel during various activities and more. Having it all tracked makes it easy to analyze your schedule and time management as a whole. This data helps you to see any areas of your life that may need improvement.

Once you have filled in your time log for a couple of days, you can utilize the information to eliminate any time-wasting activities. You may not have realized how long you actually spend on social media. Have you made note of the time you spend binge-watching your favorite television shows? You may not have realized how much time you spend gossiping by the water cooler. Activities like these are time wasters and steal your productivity and happiness. Like I've mentioned in the past, they can create more anxiety and stress in your life.

Your time log will also allow you to clearly see what time(s) of the day you are most productive and efficient. You can then be sure to schedule your most important activities or hardest work during those times when your energy level is the highest and you are most alert. Another benefit to tracking, reviewing, and analyzing a time log is that you may see a new way to batch certain tasks. As an Achievement Coach, tracking your time is essential to creating the systems and life management skills that move you closer to accomplishing your goals.

This process allows you to take a step back and see an overview of how your time is truly spent throughout the day; it allows you to take in the big picture and notice patterns or habits you may not have realized were forming.

You can eliminate any time-wasting activities. You can also cut back on – or delegate – any activities that have low importance. You may find that you have more time in your day than you originally thought, and you will be prepared to use the time to your advantage.

Completing this exercise and adjusting your schedule accordingly will help you to gain more time, be more productive, and boost your happiness levels.

It's all about being intentional with your time...with your decisions...and your life.

CHAPTER 16

ARE YOU BEING INTENTIONAL WITH YOUR TIME? A TIME LOG CAN HELP JOURNAL ACTIVITY

*E*xercise from: Are You Being Intentional with Your Time? A Time Log Can Help

Create a Time Log to record your activities for a couple of days or a week if you dare!

Sunday

- 1 am

- 2 am

- 3 am

- 4 am

- 5 am

- 6 am

- 7 am

- 8 am

- 9 am

- 10 am

- 11 am

- noon

- 1 pm

- 2 pm

- 3 pm

- 4 pm

- 5 pm

- 6 pm

- 7 pm

- 8 pm

- 9 pm

- 10 pm

- 11 pm

- 12 pm

Monday

- 1 am

- 2 am

- 3 am

- 4 am

- 5 am

- 6 am

- 7 am

- 8 am

- 9 am

- 10 am

- 11 am

- noon

- 1 pm

- 2 pm

- 3 pm

- 4 pm

- 5 pm

- 6 pm

- 7 pm

- 8 pm

- 9 pm

- 10 pm

- 11 pm

- 12 pm

Tuesday

- 1 am

- 2 am

- 3 am

- 4 am

- 5 am

- 6 am
- 7 am
- 8 am
- 9 am
- 10 am
- 11 am
- noon
- 1 pm
- 2 pm
- 3 pm
- 4 pm
- 5 pm
- 6 pm
- 7 pm
- 8 pm
- 9 pm
- 10 pm
- 11 pm
- 12 pm

Wednesday

- 1 am
- 2 am
- 3 am

- 4 am

- 5 am

- 6 am

- 7 am

- 8 am

- 9 am

- 10 am

- 11 am

- noon

- 1 pm

- 2 pm

- 3 pm

- 4 pm

- 5 pm

- 6 pm

- 7 pm

- 8 pm

- 9 pm

- 10 pm

- 11 pm

- 12 pm

Thursday

- 1 am

LISA MCGRATH

- 2 am
- 3 am
- 4 am
- 5 am
- 6 am
- 7 am
- 8 am
- 9 am
- 10 am
- 11 am
- noon
- 1 pm
- 2 pm
- 3 pm
- 4 pm
- 5 pm
- 6 pm
- 7 pm
- 8 pm
- 9 pm
- 10 pm
- 11 pm
- 12 pm

Friday

- 1 am

- 2 am

- 3 am

- 4 am

- 5 am

- 6 am

- 7 am

- 8 am

- 9 am

- 10 am

- 11 am

- noon

- 1 pm

- 2 pm

- 3 pm

- 4 pm

- 5 pm

- 6 pm

- 7 pm

- 8 pm

- 9 pm

- 10 pm

- 11 pm
- 12 pm

Saturday

- 1 am
- 2 am
- 3 am
- 4 am
- 5 am
- 6 am
- 7 am
- 8 am
- 9 am
- 10 am
- 11 am
- noon
- 1 pm
- 2 pm
- 3 pm
- 4 pm
- 5 pm
- 6 pm
- 7 pm
- 8 pm

- 9 pm

- 10 pm

- 11 pm

- 12 pm

A House With Four Rooms advocates for spending time in each of your four rooms daily to be a complete person.

1. What part of your day is always available, even if it's just a short window? More importantly, how can you protect it and nourish it in the process of reconnecting or reinventing yourself? Make a note of your answer.

----

2. What patterns have you discovered after analyzing your Time Log?

----

3. What activities did you do in your physical, mental, emotional, and spiritual rooms each day?

-
-
-
-
-
-
-
-
-
-
-
-
-
-
-
-
-
-
-

~

CHAPTER 17

THE PHYSICAL ROOM

*B*ecause I'm actively working on recovery from some health issues, I've decided to begin with a closer look at my *Physical Room*. My *Physical Room* does not consist of only exercise, but it encompasses so much more. But I can address the issue of exercise straight away; I don't have a regular exercise routine, but walking seems to fit the bill. I monitor the number of steps I take each day; my goal is to reach 10,000 steps per day and it begins with a morning walk. I typically walk for about 45 minutes at a moderate pace and get around 5000 steps to start my day. For the rest of the day, I take the stairs whenever possible, park further away from the entrance than necessary, and stand every hour or so. On the weekends, I often go out for a few hours on a variety of hiking trails, some for elevation and views and others for distance. This practice has been beneficial for many reasons, including preparing me for the Camino de Santiago trek from St. Jean Pied de Port in France to Santiago, Spain.

I have had two great experiences on the Camino de Santiago, the ancient pilgrimage across Spain, the first time in 2012 and more recently, in 2017. Preparing for my Camino adventures helped me to realize that walking and hiking is an exercise that picks up and travels with me. I can walk almost anywhere, and a walking routine allows not only for exercise, but it helps alleviate stress. I can certainly incorporate this into my daily schedule, but it has been more difficult to get out to the trails now that I'm not officially preparing for a Camino. I need to make time for it.

Another matter of circumstance in my *Physical Room* is food. I love food! I consider pasta high on my list of favorites. I love it so much that I paired it with my love for travel and spent some time in Italy taking cooking classes and learning about Sustainability on a Tuscan Farm at Tenuta di Spannocchia, an *agriturismos,* providing farm-stay accommodations about twelve miles southwest of Siena. This is where I first heard about the "farm to table" philosophy, and I learned a lot about conservation and sustainability. I continue to see a lot of things about urban gardens and living with a garden-to-table philosophy lately. After seeing the impressive gardens of the 12th-century Tuscan farm Spannocchia and eating the fresh food, I realized even more that this is a healthy philosophy. Growing your own food allows for a nutritious diet that helps fortify the physical body and mind. Lately, my unconscious life seems to be of the "fast food" variety, everything is done quickly. So when it comes to food, the Slow Food Movement intrigues me. This is something I will investigate further.

The *Physical Room* is also where I must review the food and methods of cooking that I typically use in my own kitchen. The quality of the ingredients is a major component to the success of a recipe. The quality of ingredients is also an indicator of good health. It isn't news that our diets should be rich in fruits and vegetables, and then there is much talk of the advantages of eating organic foods and the dangers of GMOs. I've also learned that it is wise and cost-effective to eat foods that are in season.

I often combine my love of reading and food by seeking out cookbooks and food in literature books. One of my favorites is

Elizabeth Romer's *The Tuscan Year*. She shares some of the traditional Italian foods that I would love to feast on. Reading this book, with the chapter divisions compiled into lists of monthly activities, foods, and chores, reminds me of the seasonal offerings that could easily make their way to my kitchen and menu. "All the year round, the produce of the farm is grown, gathered and stored following a pattern laid down centuries ago. The days begin early, end late and there are no holidays. As Silvana often observes, if you want to eat genuine food then you must work hard to make it" (Romer 4).

So, how do I bring this philosophy into my kitchen? I believe it all begins with taking an inventory of what is housed in my cupboards, refrigerator, and freezer. Eliminating processed foods and committing to fresh ingredients and whole foods. It means consuming lean proteins, meal planning, and making the desired foods easily available and within reach. It means changing my regular visits to Five Guys, Red Robin, and Bojangles to occasional ones. It means going into my *Physical Room* every single day and doing what's necessary to support my physical health.

The *Physical Room* also includes the physical space in which we live. For me, I spend a lot of time in my home office working. I like to surround myself with things that make me smile, bring back memories, and inspire me to keep doing my best.

When looking at your physical space, does it invite you in? Are you happy to spend time in your space or does it overwhelm you? Clutter is an example of overwhelm.

I invite you to reflect on how you spend time in your *physical room* and evaluate what's working and what needs to change for a healthier you and healthier lifestyle. In what ways do you "air out" your *Physical Room*?

Remember, you don't have to spend a great deal of time in your physical room, but you must go in daily to at least open a window to "air" it out.

In the meantime, I'm going to continue to reflect on my own life by taking my 24 oz. bottle of water and head out for a quick walk in the beautiful Northwest.

~

VISITING MY PHYSICAL ROOM

"Preparing for my Camino adventures helped me to realize that walking and hiking is an exercise that picks up and travels with me. I can walk almost anywhere, and a walking routine allows not only for exercise, but it helps alleviate stress."

I enjoyed seeing the markers along the route and keeping track of distances as I made my way to the Cathedral in Santiago.

CHAPTER 18

MY TOP 10 TIPS FOR PHYSICAL WELLBEING

S o, let's take a look at my top 10 physical well-being tips that are fabulous for "airing" out your *Physical Room*.

1. Eat a varied and balanced diet

People talk a lot about eating a balanced diet. That means a diet that includes elements from all of the major food groups. That's a good start, but it's not quite enough. You also need to have variety within those food groups.

Different foods contain different nutrients that your body needs to carry out its many vital processes. For example, eating fruits and vegetables is important but suppose you eat no fruits or vegetables other than carrots and apples. Your body will still not be getting all of the nutrients that it needs, so be sure to eat different foods within each food group.

Some of us have specific food restrictions and must follow a certain diet. For myself, I have to avoid Vitamin K foods, but I do include mushrooms, squashes, onions, garlic, and beets in my weekly meal planning.

2. Stay active

Staying active is extremely important. It helps to burn fat, yes, but it does so much more. Staying active is also good for your heart and your lungs, and it helps your body to keep using energy the way that it is supposed to.

After experiencing some health issues, I've learned a lot about keeping my body healthy; I have to keep it moving! Walking is my go-to exercise, but I also use a stationary bike and elliptical. I have also learned that lifting weights and practicing balancing exercises are essential to wellness.

Staying active also helps you to age gracefully. After a certain age, we start to gradually lose muscle and bone mass. Staying active in old age can help to slow these losses. There's a lot of benefits to being healthy when you're younger because it can give you a head start as you approach an advanced age. I know I wish I had started at an earlier age, especially so I could have the flexibility and balance needed for each day.

3. Stay hydrated

Staying hydrated is important. A good benchmark goal is to drink a glass of water at each meal and one between each meal. Water is usually recommended, but keep in mind that other beverages like milk and fruit juices count too.

Be careful about counting other beverages, however. Coffees and teas contain caffeine, while wine, beer, and spirits contain alcohol. Caffeine and alcohol cause your body to release fluids, so drinking too much of these liquids can actually leave your body more dehydrated.

When you wake up, your body has been fasting all night long, so you need to replenish with a glass of water. I have my first glass before I have my morning coffee by adding a slice of lemon to hot water. It's refreshing and helps my body stay hydrated.

4. Get plenty of sleep

Sleep can tend to take a backseat to work or to play, which is unfortunate. When you're asleep, your body does a number of important functions, like processing memories and repairing wear-and-tear from the day.

That's why running low on sleep for a night can leave you feeling groggy, but if you are running low on sleep for much longer, it can leave you physically exhausted.

It's important to establish nighttime rituals that signal your body and prepare it for rest. You may have to cut out eating and drinking, screen time, or television at an earlier time; some people use nightshades, recharge cell phones, and store alarm clocks away from the bed to eliminate all light sources.

5. Manage your stress

You may be thinking, "isn't this chapter about *physical* wellness tips?" It is, but when you feel stressed, your body releases chemical signals that change the way that your body runs. That means that if you're too stressed too often, it can take a toll on your physical health. Too much stress changes things like how your body uses energy, how much or how well you sleep at night, and many other factors, so find a healthy way to relax.

6. Practice moderation

A lot of things that we think of as being healthy can be unhealthy if you get too much of them. Some diets can help you lose weight in the short term but not provide adequate nutrients in the long term.

Too much exercise can mean that your body doesn't have the time and resources to build and repair itself, potentially leading to injury. The list goes on and on.

Similarly, a lot of things that we think of as unhealthy can have health benefits from time to time. Beer has chemicals that are good for the bacteria in your stomach and wine is a source of antioxidants. Even sweets have their place, as long as you don't eat too much too often.

7. Keep in touch with a healthcare provider

Your healthcare provider can help you to keep your health on track by working with you to build diet and exercise goals that work for you. They are also able to spot diseases and other potential issues well before the average individual can.

In my case, my dental hygienist and dentist mentioned something about my teeth and gums that ultimately saved my life when I mentioned what they had said to the nurse at my podiatrist appointment. Through my experience, I learned the importance of keeping regular health appointments.

8. Keep in touch with your friends

Similar to the tip on stress, one might think that this tip is out of place. Having friends provides a number of physical benefits, however. They help to lower stress levels, increase immune strength, can contribute to staying active, and can help you to make good decisions.

Friends are important: they can make you laugh, you'll share memories together, and they'll offer a shoulder and ear when you need to cry or talk.

9. Keep in touch with yourself

People who really stay in touch with themselves don't need most of the tips in this chapter, but most people don't stay really in touch with themselves. Self-awareness is important to physical wellness. Every now and then, take a quiet moment to ask yourself how you are feeling.

Are you stressed? Are you thirsty, hungry, or tired? Maybe you feel poorly and don't know why. I have some friends that are so in tune with their bodies, that they know when something isn't quite right.

Whatever your body is telling you, listen and act on it; you are likely to feel and live healthier.

10. Clean up your physical space

Your physical space should be welcoming and relaxing, at the very least, it should be organized so that you can accomplish your goals. Many studies have shown that clutter can cause chaos, overwhelm, and inaction. Just as perfectionism and procrastination can set you back from accomplishing your intended goals.

Make it a practice to clean your kitchen sink and shelves daily, wipe down your bathroom fixtures, sweep or vacuum your floors, and make your bed. Put together a plan for decluttering all areas of your house. All of these chores add a great deal to your physical wellbeing.

If you own a home, do regular maintenance inside and outside. Keep your walkways and lawn groomed. Make the entrance a cheery place to welcome your guests. It's also a good idea to stay organized, put things away, and keep your environment safe.

In all of human history, information has never been more readily available than it is right now. Most of the information I've shared in these tips is readily available and very general information. If there was something that you didn't understand or something that you did understand but want to know more about, look it up.

Take the time to schedule wellness into your life by making doctor appointments, blocking out time for exercise, and planning activities with family and friends. Learn what your body needs and take the time and interest to make sure you're taking care of yourself. Create physical spaces that help you relax, feel loved, and valued.

CHAPTER 19

THE PHYSICAL ROOM JOURNAL ACTIVITY

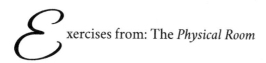xercises from: The *Physical Room*

1. When looking at your physical space, does it invite you in?

_____

_____

_____

_____

_____

_____

_____

_____

_____

2. Reflect on how you spend time in your *Physical Room* and evaluate what's working and what needs to change for a healthier you and healthier lifestyle. In what ways do you "air out" your *Physical Room*? What changes do you want to make?

_____

_____

_____

_____

_____

_____

_____

_____

_____

_____

_____

_____

_____

_____

_____

_____

∾

CHAPTER 20

THE MENTAL/INTELLECTUAL ROOM

*M*y *Mental/Intellectual Room* is a room I spend a great deal of time; I tend to "overthink" everything. It is my habit to read each morning for approximately an hour. I read several different types of materials, and I do my best reading in the morning. My ritual is to have coffee and read. This habit started many years ago when I made a New Year's resolution to read a book a week. I wanted to make sure I was investigating new ideas; it was my desire to learn about many things, and I found I could do this by reading something every day. I often read newspapers and articles online; I tend to have a novel or memoir by my chair, and I have a stack of magazines and daily devotions that I "visit" each day. I never really thought of myself as being curious, but I do have a thirst to know things. I think this is a good routine, and I benefit from this strategy.

My children are the same way; they read every day (it is true that children adopt behaviors that are modeled for them). As they were growing up, I repeated my belief that as humans, we are lifelong learners. My home has always had a room dedicated to books, and they overflow into all the other rooms of the house. We are surrounded. Now that my children have moved into their own homes, they too have surrounded themselves with books. Our collections are not limited to any one subject; we each have a thirst for knowledge, entertainment, and enlightenment.

Reading isn't the only way one goes into the *Mental Room*. Taking classes and exploring new interests is a way to continue learning. I believe education isn't limited to the four walls of a school building; there are many opportunities to engage all learners. Distance education and traveling have a purpose. I've done both, and I will continue to take classes and travel because there is so much to learn and do.

A visit to my *Mental Room* includes a host of other opportunities, such as conversations with interesting people and the sharing of ideas and thoughts. I listen to podcasts and read blogs. These activities have added to my curiosity and motivated me to write my own lifestyle blog, *Stepping Stones*. My blogging experience is challenging while navigating the website, finding a theme, learning about categories and tags, and trying to figure out how to make links; it's been confusing, but I'm persevering. I enjoy the reflective practice of writing and learning new things. I'm comfortable with the idea that my *Mental Room* gets sufficiently aired.

In what ways do you "air out" your *Mental Room*? Remember, "airing out" this room includes expanding your positive thoughts, learning new things, practicing your skills, having great conversations, and monitoring and decluttering any negative thoughts.

~

CHAPTER 21

MY TOP 10 TIPS FOR WELLBEING IN THE MENTAL ROOM

I have followed Dr. Daniel Amen for a couple of years and really found his PBS shows, books, and website to be informative about brain health. When we take care of our brain health, we are in alignment with the philosophy of the Indian Proverb *A House With Four Rooms* that suggests it is important to go into each of your four rooms (physical, mental, emotional, and spiritual rooms) each day to at least "air" them out. Many of the activities, strategies, and tips that I'm offering in this book and my coaching programs actually help you "air" out more than one room at a time.

These tips do just that: they overlap the other rooms and allow you multiple benefits.

1. Eat a Balanced And Varied Diet, Monitor Carbs, and Eat the Right Fats

A lot of the tips on this list sound like they belong on a list of tips for physical health. Your mental health, however, is dependent on the health of your brain, which is part of your body. What you put into your body has a strong impact on your mental health.

LISA MCGRATH

Chemicals from a great many foods are used directly by your brain or are used to create chemicals that influence how your brain works. As a result, if your diet is too limited, it might be limiting your mind.

Calcium and potassium are key examples. These ions are important in handling electrical charges that allow your nerves to communicate with each other and with your body. Run low on them and you may feel sluggish.

My friend, Dawn, is a huge advocate for growing your own fruits and veggies, and she has her own chickens for fresh eggs. She avoids GMO foods and chooses to eat "clean".

Your body can burn carbohydrates, fats, and proteins for fuel. Your brain, however, is only able to run on the energy released from carbohydrates and fats. That means that if you try to cut fats and carbs out of your diet as some extreme diets recommend, you may be getting enough nutrients to power your muscles, but your brain might be running behind.

Just make sure to get your carbs from healthy sources like fruits and whole grains rather than from processed grains and sweets.

As mentioned above, fat is metabolized for brain fuel. That's not the only way in which fat is important to your brain, however.

Your brain and key components of the rest of your nervous system are made primarily out of fat. Fat in your nervous system works as an electrical insulator to help keep electrical signals in your body running the way that they should. Successfully avoid fats for too long, and your brain will notice.

Just be sure to get your fat from healthy sources such as walnuts, avocados, fatty fish, and olive or nut oils. It is possible to make better choices at the grocery store and in your daily diet. I also like to create a menu plan that I can rely on when I go to the grocery store; it only takes a few minutes to fill out a grocery list when you create a simple checklist of all of your favorite foods.

2. Moderation Of Alcohol

As mentioned above, your brain is made primarily of fat. Alcohol is a solvent capable of dissolving fat. Your liver can only filter alcohol at a rate of about one standard drink per hour. After that, it starts to circulate in your blood. Drink too heavy too often, and it can cause permanent damage. Remember, to drink responsibly, learn more, and seek advice from your doctor.

3. Keep Your Body Active

Your brain needs oxygen and other nutrients, which are brought to your brain by your blood. Your blood is pumped by your heart, but it's helped along by muscles. This is especially true of blood in your lower body.

Here your body needs to work against gravity to get blood from areas like your legs back up to the heart and lungs. That's why if you sit for too long you can lose focus. I make it a habit to get up and move at least every hour, and when I get on an airplane, I pump my legs and wear compression stockings to help keep my blood moving.

When you are physically active, you also take in more oxygen. This helps your muscles, but it also helps your brain. The next time you need to "jog your memory" try actually jogging and see if that helps.

4. Keep Your Brain Active

Your brain doesn't work exactly like a muscle, but the "use it or lose it" mentality should be the same. To keep your wits sharp, use them often by playing word, number, and logic-based games.

Reading and learning new things is a great way to keep your brain active. This is very important for "airing" out your Mental Room.

5. Keep In Touch With Your Friends

Crosswords and sudokus aren't the only way to keep your brain sharp. Chatting with other people can encourage you to think about new ideas and to think of them in new ways. Any time that your brain is being challenged, it is growing.

Your friends have the ability to listen to you and share in your life; often, your friends will keep you grounded and in touch with reality.

Deep and thoughtful conversations are a way to "air out" your mental room as you use critical and analytical thinking skills to participate.

6. Keep In Touch With Yourself and Expand Your Mind

Mental health problems like memory loss and other conditions have a way of sneaking up on people. Every now and then, take a few moments to check in with how you are feeling. Are you able to remember things, including names and important dates?

Do you often find yourself confused while carrying out tasks and conversations? If so, it may be important to talk to a healthcare provider.

Make sure to stay organized and read often to expand your thoughts and knowledge. Try to keep your thoughts positive, curious, and active.

As mentioned above, your healthcare provider can be an important resource if you think that something is wrong with your mental health. Also, as mentioned above, your mental health is closely tied to your physical health. By helping you to stay physically healthy, your doctor is helping you to maintain your mental health as well.

Mindfulness is about monitoring your thoughts and being self-aware of your habits, too. What are you learning? What skills are you practicing?

7. Keep Reading and Learning

Your brain craves information. You can also do more research on some of the topics discussed in this chapter so that you can improve your mental health and keep your brain going strong for as long as possible.

You can do this in short bursts each day by reading new materials, setting time aside for learning, conversing, and doing...practice new skills, take a class, or subscribe to some YouTube presenters.

An essential part of my morning routine includes reading. I have several books that I "visit" each day. I typically read a chapter or two, a devotion, and ponder points I research. This is a valuable practice for me and without it, I don't think my day would be the same.

8. Take Up a New Skill

There are always new things to learn and do. Have you ever wanted to learn a new language? Perhaps take up golf, join the local theatre, or any number of other skill-building opportunities. Explore the possibilities and stretch yourself and your mind.

9. Be Creative

Perhaps it's time to write your autobiography or a novel. Explore the arts, whether you pick up a paintbrush or visit an art museum. If you have littles at home, take them into the kitchen and bake some cookies that you can decorate. Try making some bread or fresh pasta. Turn up the music and have a private dance party. Take some time to create a personal masterpiece.

10. Travel to Learn about New Places, People, and Things

If you can't physically visit new places, go to the local library and get some travel books and videos to watch about faraway places. Where in the world would you like to go? What foods would you be having? Who are the people that you'd meet? How would you spend your time? What places would you visit?

An alternative is to explore your own town or city. What can you learn about the place where you live and work? Try interviewing some of the older community members to get a feel for what "home" used to be like and how much it has changed. The idea is to continue learning.

How do you "air" out your *Mental Room*? Are you learning something new? Taking a class? Learning an instrument?

Find ways to "air" out your rooms as prescribed by the Indian Proverb. The benefits are essential to all domains of your life. You will quickly see the rewards for your efforts because everything you do spills into all areas of your life.

∾

CHAPTER 22

THE MENTAL/INTELLECTUAL ROOM JOURNAL ACTIVITY

*E*xercise from: The *Mental/Intellectual Room*

1. In what ways do you "air out" your *Mental Room*? Remember, "airing out" this room includes expanding your positive thoughts, learning new things, practicing your skills, having great conversations, and monitoring and decluttering any negative thoughts.

----

2. Reflect on how you spend time in your *Mental Room* and evaluate what's working and what needs to change for a healthier you and healthier lifestyle. In what ways do you "air out" your mental room? What changes do you want to make?

_____

_____

_____

_____

_____

_____

_____

_____

_____

_____

_____

_____

_____

_____

_____

_____

∽

CHAPTER 23

THE EMOTIONAL ROOM

*T*oday I'm addressing the *Emotional Room.* As for my *Emotional Room*, I think, like many people, I've tried to avoid it on most occasions to avoid disappointments, hard feelings, and general sadness and melancholy. I believe most of us try to deal and cope to the best of our abilities, while others have a more difficult time and seem to get "locked" out of this room without the strength of going in to open a window to "air" it out. I've learned if I focus on the moments, and I go into "air" out the *Emotional Room*, my life seems easier. I have taught myself some coping strategies that work for me: journaling helps sift through thoughts and reminds me of my blessings, remembering "what other people think of me is none of my business" lets me be me, and knowing that I cannot control others but I can choose how I respond helps me make decisions.

Sometimes it is difficult to deny the personal hardships and forget the blessings, so keeping a journal helps me put feelings and events in perspective. I have kept journals off and on for most of my life. I have daily journals, travel journals, and gratitude journals. I find it remarkable that something extraordinary will happen and I tell myself, "I'll never forget this," only to find myself reminded by the event only when I go back and read it in a journal. Many of my daily journals document both hard times and happy times, but the difficult times seem to dominate. I find myself journaling in order to relieve stress and help me sort things out. When things are going well, I seem to fall out of the habit of writing as consistently in the daily journals.

My travel journals are fantastic for remembering some of the details of wondrous trips I've been fortunate to take. Europe is my favorite destination, with England, Italy, and Spain at the top of my favorites list. Each time I visit a place, I learn new things and build new memories by remaining open to the opportunities that enrich my life.

Gratitude journals help keep life authentic; I've kept a gratitude journal for years and have given lessons on keeping a gratitude journal. To keep things simple, I suggest writing down five things every single day that you are grateful for. This practice is particularly good for times when one just wants to crawl into bed and pull the covers up. Besides, if you make a commitment to writing five things down each day, you must get up out of bed to face the day and find those things. Sometimes, I admit, I've had days that I have looked back on previous blessings to help come up with my five, but most often, I have more than five and the number of blessings can carry on for pages.

The advice that "what other people think of you is none of your business" has been valuable to me throughout my life. As a child, I learned that I could not let someone else's opinion and words dictate my life. When I was told I wasn't good enough or wouldn't amount to anything, I stood steadfast and was determined to prove the naysayers wrong. It can be difficult when these thoughts and words are supplied by people within your circle of authority, the same people you are meant to trust and whose opinions you want to value. Well, after many years of teaching and hearing similar stories to my own, I've learned that it is important to be realistic and determine whose opinions you value.

Brené Brown suggests writing the names of all the people that love and support you unconditionally, imperfections and all, on a 1x1 inch piece of paper. When you are confronted by a review or judgment that seems hurtful or misguided, take a look at that paper and see if the source is listed. If not, move forward and away from the nonsense. Feedback is a necessary tool for growth when given and used appropriately, but one must live with intention and make decisions with and be guided by all facts and many naysayers don't have all the facts or they only have their interpretation of the facts, so their opinions are careless and limited.

I learned early on that the business of my life is my business, so it is important to be my own CEO and to know that my true power is knowing that I choose how I respond to outside triggers. Triggers are events, situations, and people that you do not have control over; remember, the only thing that is in your control is how you choose to respond in every moment.

We are not marionette masters that control others. There have been many times that emotions well up so quickly that I haven't had a chance to "think" about how I want to respond; the danger of this for me is that the emotions can sometimes create a knee-jerk reaction and my decision-making process becomes foggy. Getting a handle on the authenticity and power of my own emotions and melding them with appropriate thoughts, attitudes, and boundaries helps me keep things in perspective. It also allows me to protect myself, especially when I feel vulnerable to outside triggers. I've also learned that I must be honest with myself and acknowledge how I feel about the triggers.

I'm learning that those I let into my circle, those with who I choose to share my thoughts and feelings, particularly when I feel the most vulnerable, are the ones whose opinions matter, not the other critics. Our lives (the good, bad, and ugly) should not be fodder for gossip for others, particularly those within our inner circle; instead, our lives should be joyous celebrations, learned lessons that we share, and grateful blessings we cherish.

The *Emotional Room* has always been a difficult room for me; it is a rollercoaster of emotional highs and lows, but I've learned it is important to recognize and acknowledge all of my feelings for the ability to move on. It's not a time to rehash the trigger or beat myself up. It's a time for learning and understanding, a time of forgiveness, and once on solid ground, a time to "make my mess my message" to help others to know there is a way to cope and deal with messes.

I'm on a quest for peace and happiness, and I'll decorate my *Emotional Room* by choosing the events and situations I expose myself to; I can walk away from gossip; I can choose how I speak to and about people; I can choose my own happiness. To accomplish this I will participate in "airing" out my rooms by spending a bit of time in each one, each day, in my own way. It is in this way that I take what I have learned from all experiences and continue on my journey.

In what ways do you "air" out your *Emotional Room?*

CHAPTER 24

MY TOP 10 EMOTIONAL WELLNESS TIPS

*T*he Indian Proverb states we should think of ourselves as *A House With Four Rooms*: physical, mental, emotional, and spiritual rooms. It advocates for going into each room every single day, not for long periods of time, but going in each day to at least "air" it out.

Most of the tips I'm sharing overlap and apply to more than one room; however, today, my focus is on emotional wellness. Here are the tips that I believe are the most important and provide the most benefit.

1. Eat A Balanced And Varied Diet

Emotions change based on what's happening around you, but they also change based on what's happening within you.

Your emotions are partially dependent on your body chemistry, which has a lot to do with what you eat. This is largely because emotions are partially controlled by hormones and other chemical messengers in the body which are constructed from chemicals that your body takes from the food that you eat. A poor diet can mean poor emotional health.

Garbage in...garbage out. Feed your body, brain, and heart with great foods.

Make sure to hydrate with plenty of water and limit caffeine and alcohol.

Your body deserves good nutrition.

2. Practice Moderation

Drinks are fine with dinner or unwinding, but if you get in the habit of using alcohol to forget your problems, it will likely just make your problems worse. Alcohol is a depressant, so it may make you feel better in the moment, too much too often can leave you feeling worse. Some experts even believe that alcohol can activate a gene that makes you more likely to develop depression.

Moderation in ALL things seems like the best plan: red meat, alcohol, exercise, television, etc. You get the idea.

3. Do Work You Love

Not just any work, work that is important to you. When many of us are at work, we feel like we'd rather just be doing nothing. The work that you do, however, can help to give you a sense of purpose and identity. This means that any work can be good work, but that you are likely to have a better mood and a better outlook on life if you are doing work that you enjoy.

I believe it's important to do the best at any and all jobs you do. From my perspective, always give them a "quarter for their dime" or in other words, do more than required or expected and make it the best you can do...always.

4. Manage Stress

Stress isn't just a feeling, it's a physiological state. When you are stressed, your body releases different amounts of chemical messengers that determine how you feel and how your body functions. Over the long term, stress can negatively impact your physical and emotional health.

Developing a Meditation Practice is a fantastic way to visit the Emotional Room because a regular practice has the ability to help you remain calm, slow your breathing, and keep you focused.

5. Have A Support Network

For everyday problems, catastrophes, or whatever gets you down, it's important to have a support network. This can be emotional support, financial support, someone to give advice, or just a shoulder to lean on.

Support networks can be networks in your community or online that are specifically for helping people who are dealing with problems like the loss of a loved one, an empty nest, and substance abuse, or they can be family and friends that support your good health and wellbeing.

A House With Four Rooms also has a Facebook page (www.facebook. com/ahousewithfourrooms) that offers inspiration, encouragement, and support.

6. Find Healthy Coping Mechanisms

Some people turn to alcohol and other drugs to help them to deal with unpleasant emotions. Almost all of the time, however, these coping mechanisms do more harm than good. Instead, try to find a hobby that makes you feel better.

Keeping a Journal, volunteering, playing an instrument, sewing, quilting, and painting are all examples of healthy coping mechanisms. It's wonderful to help others and forget about your own stress for a while.

7. Have Faith

A study released a few years ago found that people who practice religion are statistically healthier than those who don't, including in terms of mental health. The study was conducted in a Christian community, but there's no reason to think that other religions don't offer the same benefits.

Religion often encourages a discussion of difficult topics like death. It also encourages hope and a focus on non-material goods. Church communities can often be sources of support in times of crisis.

8. Have Friends

As mentioned above, friends can be an important component in support networks. Friends aren't only good for helping you through bad times, they are also good for a good time.

Having a few good friends can help you to feel appreciated and can help introduce you to new interests and pastimes.

9. Stay In Touch With Your Feelings

Paying attention to your feelings can help you to address them as they appear rather than letting them build up. Feelings that aren't processed in an appropriate and timely manner can often develop into stronger and stronger emotions that are difficult to deal with in a healthy and productive way.

Be self-aware and set personal and professional boundaries that support your well-being.

10. Keep in Touch With Your Healthcare Provider

As mentioned above, your emotional wellness is at least partially reliant on your physical wellness. By helping you to stay physically healthy, your doctor can help you to stay emotionally healthy.

Professionals are available for every domain of your life; you do not have to journey this life alone. Reach out and maintain a healthy lifestyle that supports your complete wellness.

Of course, if you find problems with your emotional health, you can also bring these up with your doctor, who may be able to offer advice, resources, or referrals to other experts.

Over the years I have had several mentors and coaches that have been essential for my emotional well-being. I've been taught, supported, and inspired to live my best life.

For more information and updates about my programs, visit my website at https://www.lisamcgrath.me.

What are you doing in your *Emotional* Room today? I hope it provides you with the greatest peace and joy!

CHAPTER 25

THE EMOTIONAL ROOM JOURNAL ACTIVITY

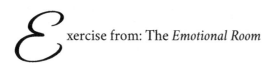xercise from: The *Emotional Room*

1. So, what are you feeling today? In what ways do you "air" out your *Emotional Room?*

----

2. Reflect on how you spend time in your *Emotional Room* and evaluate what's working and what needs to change for a healthier you and healthier lifestyle. In what ways do you "air out" your *Emotional Room*? What changes do you want to make?

~

CHAPTER 26

THE SPIRITUAL ROOM

*M*y *Spiritual Room* includes my rituals of praying and meditation, and I participate in spiritual development as a member of my church. I also believe in random acts of kindness and try to use these acts as a way of spiritual practice. I delight in the wonders of nature: the beautiful sunrises, sunsets, and scenes of life, so I enjoy attending what I fondly call "The Church of the Great Blue Dome" when I can. I like to walk while I meditate or pray; I like to count my blessings and practice gratitude.

In the last chapter, I spoke about different journaling practices. Over the years, I've kept a gratitude journal. This journal is dedicated to writing down the blessings of the day. It is my intention to write down five things each day that I am grateful for; from my experience, there have been many days that I can write down much more than the prerequisite five; however, there have been other days that I have to go back and read over prior lists to help come up with my five things. I find this a spiritual activity, and it reminds me of my abundant blessings.

Another example of my spiritual practice includes reading. I try to read every day. I have a stack of books on my nightstand that I "visit" each morning and others for the evening. I read devotionals, spiritual texts, nonfiction, self-help, and fiction. This practice gives me a focus for my meditations, shapes my thinking, and guides my life.

Visiting nature, art museums, churches, and other places is included in my worship and wonderful additions to "airing" my own *Spiritual Room*. It is simply a matter of taking the time to incorporate the activities and practices into a daily schedule and soon rituals are established. One of the most valuable practices for me is meditation, and I would like to devote even more time to meditation.

It is the practice of social connection that brings me to worship with like-minded others. It is this commonality that makes the everyday ordinary extraordinary. The social connection allows me to feel like I am not alone in my pursuit of faith, spirituality, and peace. In his book *Simple Prosperity*, Dave Wann states, "By changing the way we regard the world, the 'me' in each of us becomes a much wider 'we,' and we feel interconnected and complete. Even in a world filled with contradiction and superficiality, we find True North" (69). Connecting to people and places expands the walls of my *Spiritual Room*.

It has been my great fortune to be "called" to walk the ancient route of pilgrims along the Camino Frances to Santiago, Finisterre, and Muxia in Spain; I have made the journey twice and eagerly look forward to returning. Both of my Camino experiences were a major part of spending time in my *Spiritual Room*. The experiences I had reminded me that the ordinary can most definitely be *extraordinary*.

During my journey, I learned many lessons and was reminded of important truths, and many of these lessons from the Camino connect to all four of my rooms. A day doesn't go by that I don't think of places I visited, of people I met, or of experiences I had on the Camino. The pilgrims travel the ancient route for many reasons, but in my mind, this pilgrimage is spiritual as one connects to self, others, and a higher power.

I'd love to hear how others "air" out their *Spiritual Rooms*. Do you have activities and rituals that bring you closer to God, the Divine, the Universe, or Higher Power?

~

VISITING MY SPIRITUAL ROOM

"A day doesn't go by that I don't think of places I visited, of people I met, or of experiences I had on the Camino. The pilgrims travel the ancient route for many reasons, but in my mind, this pilgrimage is spiritual as one connects to self, others, and a higher power."

My pilgrimage didn't end in Santiago; matter of fact, I believe each day continues my journey and my personal *pilgrimage to self*.

CHAPTER 27

MY TOP 10 TIPS FOR SPIRITUAL WELLNESS

*W*hen it comes to wellness, taking care of your body, mind, and emotions does not encompass all that you are. Tending to your spirit is just as important as the other pieces and can bring you tremendous satisfaction and peace. Your spiritual wellness includes your sense of purpose and meaning in life as well as the guiding principles behind your thoughts and actions.

How can you improve your spiritual wellness? By implementing daily practices into your life, you "air" out your *Spiritual Room*. You will need to explore strategies to find ones that work best for you and your needs, but here are my top ten spiritual wellness tips to get you started.

1. Practice Gratitude

Being grateful for what you have in life that brings you joy and peace is a wonderful way to recognize your own values. In my course, *Developing a Gratitude Practice*, I suggest taking time each day to acknowledge your gratitude by recording your appreciation or blessing in a gratitude journal. Another great way is to send thank-you notes or messages to others who contribute to your spiritual growth and health. Acknowledging your gratitude and blessings invites you into welcoming even more. Your life is abundant in many ways.

2. Get to Know Your Spiritual Core

Understanding what drives you as a person and what brings meaning to your life is essential to spiritual wellness. Reflect on your values, your purpose, and your identity regularly to ensure you are aligning your beliefs with your behaviors and feel confident in your choices. Regular reflection helps you recognize and address problems in your spirituality before they become too large to manage. Make it a practice to check in with your thoughts, feelings, and actions.

3. Work On Self-Acceptance

Tending to your spirit means being comfortable with who you are and what you believe. Accepting that you are unique in this world and that you don't have to agree with or be like anyone else means you are confident in your mission and choices in life. You have the right to know and feel your authentic self, have self-love, and the confidence to live your truth. Take 100% responsibility for your life: your thoughts, feelings, and actions belong to you.

4. Explore the World

Exploring the world, even if it's just within your own community, helps you appreciate the diversity of thoughts and ideas in our society. I believe it's important to take advantage of opportunities to travel because it's a great way to get you out of your comfort zone, which is often the best place to identify your real values and needs in life, too. Make it a habit to explore the world and learn about people and places.

5. Be More Mindful

Living in the moment teaches you to appreciate life and all its everyday pleasures and curiosities. Paying full attention brings you into harmony with your environment and others and allows you to stay more connected to yourself and your needs, too. Being self-aware and mindful allows you to stay in the moment and focused and is an essential practice to living an *Intentional Life.*

6. Explore the Deeper Meanings

When you see recurring patterns in your life, dig a little deeper. What do these patterns tell you about your values, beliefs, and behaviors? How can you use this understanding to enhance your spirit and control your path forward? Awareness of these deeper meanings can help you feel happier and more at peace in life. You do not have to adopt the values, beliefs, and behaviors of others; you must develop and connect to your own.

7. Focus on the Positive

Thinking positively lifts your spirits as well as helps you consider alternatives to problems. Positivity helps you focus on what you want to achieve and what brings you joy and satisfaction in life, as well. Reframing your thoughts to be more positive is one way to enhance your spiritual wellness every day.

8. Express Yourself

When you keep emotions or thoughts bottled up, it can cloud your mind and leave you feeling unsatisfied. Writing your feelings down or talking about them with a trusted partner or friend can help you clarify what is bothering you and how this connects to your values and beliefs. Remember, your feelings are created by your thoughts, so as stated above, reframe your thoughts to be more positive and smile...it has the power to change your emotions.

9. Try Yoga, Prayer, and Meditation

These activities are both based on mindfulness practices that reduce stress as well as emotional and physical strain, which can block your spiritual growth. These practices focus on teaching you to listen to your body, to quiet your mind, and to be present at the moment, all of which are healthy for your spiritual growth and development. My belief is when you pray, you are doing the talking, and when you meditate, you are listening for the "God Whispers".

10. Give Back

Giving back to others through donating time, money, or even blood can provide you with ways to align your values with your actions. Volunteering gives you a direct outlet to support your spiritual needs by attending to the needs of others in many ways.

It's a magical process when you act out of love and service without expectations of something in return. It allows your spirit to shine, align with your core values, and personal beliefs.

As a spiritual being, you have the power to live an extraordinary life! What are you doing to "air" out your *Spiritual Room*?

Do you have a practice of going into your four rooms daily?

CHAPTER 28

LIVING WITH PURPOSE IS GOOD FOR YOUR SPIRITUAL HEALTH

*T*he philosophy of *A House With Four Rooms* is to live with purpose...to live your *Intentional Life* and spiritual health or wellness and the effect living with purpose has on it. It doesn't matter what your own spirituality or religion is. We live in a very diverse society and as a result, some of my readers will have different beliefs than others. Even within a group of people from the same faith or belief system, there are fast differences between individual faiths or spiritual beliefs. In the end, living with purpose and intention is beneficial, no matter what you believe.

Having a purpose is a primal human need. We want to be needed and we need to know that we're making a difference in order to feel fulfilled, happy, and complete. That's why living with purpose is so important and why it is good for your overall spiritual health.

We like to be needed by others. It makes us sad and lonely when we can't help those around us and make a difference in their lives. Having a purpose and living with purpose allows us to do just that on a regular basis. It fulfills our need to be needed.

Another common human desire or need is to find meaning in life. We don't like to feel like we're wasting our time here. Living with purpose gives meaning to each day. That, in turn, makes us feel happier and more fulfilled.

At the end of the day, even when things seem bad, we need to have hope. Having a purpose means we have a plan and we have something to strive towards. There's hope there. It is hoped that we'll make a difference, it is hoped that things will get better, and it is hoped that we can get ourselves out of the hole we find ourselves in.

We also need values to live a happy and fulfilled life. Our values are like a compass that guides us along the way. If you are a parent, you know how important it is to impart strong values to your children. Without them, they feel lost and insecure. That can add a lot of stress and unhappiness. We're no different as adults. Living our life with purpose by default provides us with a strong set of values to live by. And it's essential to discover your own purpose, determine your own values, and develop your own beliefs.

Living with purpose is good for the mind and spirit. It allows you to live a more fulfilling and happier life and make a difference in the world.

The philosophy of the Indian Proverb, *A House With Four Rooms*, is to do something daily for your physical, mental, emotional, and spiritual health for overall wellness. There are many ways to visit your *Spiritual Room;* some of my favorite ways are my daily rituals that include meditation, prayer, and reading morning devotionals including reading from *The Daily Word* a Unity Publication.

I have a prayer practice that includes giving thanks throughout my day. I also have a special *prayer book* that I pray with; in it, I've written the first names of family, friends, and acquaintances that have requested prayer.

When I walk, I do a dedicated prayer and a meditation walk. The practices that you include in your daily life not only aid the global universe but raise your own vibration. Spending time in your *Spiritual Room* allows you to experience a sense of peace.

Some other tips to "air" out your *Spiritual Room* include:

- light a candle
- listen to inspirational music, hymns, and chants
- try a meditation technique
- pray
- commune in nature
- write in a spiritual journal
- reading

There are many ways you can choose to "air out" your rooms, and one of the benefits, whatever you choose to do, has the ability to spill over into the other areas. Everything you do allows you to build a strong foundation as you move closer to achieving your goals and living your *Intentional Life.*

CHAPTER 29

THE SPIRITUAL ROOM JOURNAL ACTIVITY

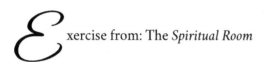 xercise from: The *Spiritual Room*

1. What were your childhood experiences around spirituality and/or religion?

_____

_____

_____

_____

_____

_____

_____

_____

_____

. . .

2. Reflect on how you spend time in your *Spiritual Room* and evaluate what's working and what needs to change for a healthier you and healthier lifestyle. In what ways do you "air out" your *Spiritual Room*? What changes do you want to make?

∾

CHAPTER 30

HERE'S WHY YOU HAVE TO BE INTENTIONAL
WITH WHAT YOU WANT IN LIFE

I'm excited to share some of the lessons from my coaching program, *A Pilgrimage to Self* in this book and grateful for all the personal messages and updates from my readers.

Living your best life involves a great number of aspects, and as most people learn, you don't have to go on this journey alone...you can get a coach, accountability partner, or tribe to help you move forward towards your dreams.

A Pilgrimage to Self takes each client on a journey within and helps keep them accountable and on track for living their best life. The goals we set are very personal and unique to each other; however, there are some common goals and strategies that can help anyone achieve what they want in life.

As an Achievement Coach, I share actions you can take to put your goals at the forefront and create actionable guidelines for reaching them. I show you how to knock out obstacles like fear and uncertainty, so you can forge ahead and become the best version of yourself.

It's so important to dream big and take risks. Too often in life, we remain in our comfort zone in an attempt to stay safe or to avoid discomfort. When you do that, you destroy any chance you have of accomplishing new heights. You hold yourself back. You might even allow others to keep you in place due to their own projections and will.

Overcoming these obstacles can seem challenging, and it will take time. You can do it and live a life beyond what you're currently experiencing. The key, however, is to know what you want. Many of us only know we want to be happier, live bigger, or shine brighter. We don't know exactly what it is that will help us reach those milestones.

That's where being *intentional* comes into play. Intentional living requires a clear picture of what you want. It's a process of creating goals and then setting achievable objectives and milestones for attaining them. To be intentional is to live each aspect of your life with your goal in mind.

You must understand the *why*, or the reason, your overall goals, and the smaller objectives that are important to you. Otherwise, you'll lack the motivation to reach them. You also need to develop an action plan of substance and clarity in order to get from point A to point B.

While this may seem intimidating right now, let me assure you that you have the tools you need to make it happen; it is my belief you'll feel empowered and ready to begin preparing to live your best life when you discover, design, and develop a plan.

CHAPTER 31

CULTIVATING A "CAN DO" MINDSET

*S*ometimes we hold ourselves back from living our best life by focusing on our limitations and those taught to us in our childhood. This is why I have my clients analyze their values and belief systems. It's important to uncover what drives you on your mission.

Often, we convince ourselves there's only so much we can do and that we can't progress further...in my case, my childhood lessons were about how I wasn't good enough or capable. And, that's actually untrue. You can almost always improve in some way. The key is to change from a fixed mindset that says this is as good as it gets to a growth mindset in which you are aware that improvement is possible. Take a look at some ways you can cultivate a "can do" mindset in order to reach your goals:

First, you'll need to shift your focus from your limitations to your potential. Instead of thinking, "I'll never be able to do that," change your mindset to consider the possibilities. Tell yourself that you may not be the very best, but you can practice and improve whatever skill it is you'd like to learn...learn the power of "yet."

When a baby is learning to walk and stumbles and falls, we don't discourage them from trying again by saying something like "You're not very good at walking...stop wasting your time." Instead, we encourage them to try again. All skills take practice. Some even report that it takes over 10,000 hours of practicing a skill to become a master. Imagine if all the successful people you can think of gave up too soon.

Fear of failure is a powerful motivator that can often hold us back. It's okay to fail. Tell yourself that failing is part of the growth process and part of getting better. Your failure doesn't define who you are. It's an essential aspect of life, and it teaches you so much...use what you learn to make improvements and develop your next best steps.

One of the techniques I love is the Japanese form of Kaizen...making small, consistent actions for constant change. These changes are enough to move you closer to your goals; it has the power to build momentum and clear the way for you to live the life you desire. There is tremendous value when you can move forward and make progress.

It's so easy to identify our weaknesses; for some reason, though, we have a hard time naming our strengths. This is something you need to overcome if you want to cultivate a "can do" mindset. Everyone has talents, skills, and positive personality traits. Get in touch with yours. Ask a trusted friend if you aren't sure what those are. When you gain confidence in your abilities, you'll be more open to experiencing growth.

My clients take different assessments to discover and connect to their strengths...knowing your strengths helps you design your next best steps towards reaching your desired goals, and knowing your strengths, relying on your strengths, has the ability to build momentum to help you move toward your goals.

Another navigational tip for your journey is learning to deal with challenges. Don't shy away from challenges. Instead, take them on with gusto. The above points should help you to overcome mental obstacles that may be holding you back. Trying something that is challenging is a surefire way to grow and to gain a wide variety of skills. You'll also be opening yourself up to some potentially wonderful experiences.

I am a firm believer that you are the author of your life...you must take the responsibility of creating your best life, but you don't have to do it alone. Find a partner, coach, or mentor to help you stay challenged and accountable.

Beware of comparing yourself to others. Comparison is a killer when it comes to self-confidence and living your best life. Don't tell yourself all the ways you're not as good as someone else. Instead, look to them for inspiration. Find ways that you can become motivated by their skill or success. Then set out to bring those characteristics to your own personal experience.

Use these tips as a guide for embracing a "can do" mindset. Pay attention to the ways in which your thought process begins to change and to the experiences you become open to having.

CELEBRATE YOUR SUCCESSES

My son and I celebrating our 500-mile trek to the end of the world: Cape Finistere, a rock-bound peninsula at the westernmost point of the Iberian Peninsula on the west coast of Galicia, Spain.

～

CHAPTER 32

CULTIVATING A "CAN DO" MINDSET JOURNAL
ACTIVITY

 xercise from: Cultivating a "Can Do" Mindset

Recognizing our individual strengths, talents, and gifts is essential to cultivating a "Can Do" Mindset; however, often, we concentrate too much on weaknesses, obstacles, and faults rather than our positive attributes. Take the time to take stock in your education, training, personal strengths, talents, and gifts.

1. Describe your education, training, personal strengths, talents, and gifts.

----

2. Make a *Bad Ass Moments* list by listing all your incredible accomplishments and proudest moments.

-
-
-
-
-
-
-
-
-
-
-
-
-
-
-
-
-
-

❧

CHAPTER 33

YOU BECOME LIKE THE PEOPLE YOU SPEND
THE MOST TIME WITH

*W*ho are the people you spend the most time with in your life? Consider the types of individuals these folks are. What types of personality traits do they exhibit? Do they behave in ways that bring positivity to your life? These are important questions to consider because the people you associate with most can have a great deal of influence on your personality and your overall well-being. This concept was first introduced to me by mentor Jim Rohn and then again through Mary Kay Ash. When you take time to ask yourself the questions, be self-aware with your time and the people you allow in your inner circle, you can begin to make changes if you're not happy with the current company you're keeping.

It was businessman Jim Rohn who once famously said, "You're the average of the five people you spend most of your time with." It makes sense that you would absorb some of the traits and attitudes of those around you. They say complaining is contagious...have you observed this? Have you ever noticed that you find yourself grumpy and negative when you're around a constant complainer? The same can be true of positivity. Just as boredom is contagious, so is attitude. When spending significant time with people who are encouraging and supportive, you'll likely find yourself exhibiting similar qualities. Who are the people you spend the most time with?

First, you'll want to assess your most common company. Who are the five people you spend the most time with? Write them down. Once you have your list, ask yourself some questions about these individuals. Who are they and for how long have they been in your life? Now, consider what each person's typical demeanor is like. Are they successful in their careers and goals? Do they pursue opportunities for regular growth? What types of activities do they do to support their personal and professional goals? Are they supportive when you're going through difficult times? Do they encourage you to be your best self? How do they respond when you share a personal or professional win?

Taking an assessment such as this of the people you surround yourself with most frequently will give you an idea as to whether you need to make some changes.

You should now have a general assessment of which people are building you up and which may be holding you back. Now you have some decisions to make. This assessment requires brutal honesty on your part, but it's an investment worth making.

Be open to change and feel free to make adjustments as you see fit. You can start by making dates to spend more time with the people who are your greatest influences and begin distancing yourself from the negative ones. Or you can make more drastic cuts if there are individuals who are truly toxic. The important thing is to be aware of how the people around you are impacting your life and to take steps to surround yourself with more positive folks.

One of the best ways to surround yourself with positive, inspiring, and encouraging people is to find your *tribe*...a group of like-minded people that want to see each other succeed. You can do this by joining Facebook groups, seeking out new people in MeetUps, and joining a coaching program. Once you do, you'll begin to uplift your attitude and accelerate your progress on your goals.

You'll start to notice a difference in your life as you make these changes. Surrounding yourself with uplifting people lightens your mood and increases your motivation. You'll simply feel better and more energized when you're proactively choosing your inner circle. How wonderful will that be?

∾

CHAPTER 34

YOU BECOME LIKE THE PEOPLE YOU SPEND
THE MOST TIME WITH

*E*xercise from: You Become Like the People You Spend the Most Time With

1. List the five people you spend the most time with and describe their character traits, values, and strengths of each. What do you admire about them? What character traits, values, and strengths do you have in common?

•

●

●

. . .

•

•

~

CHAPTER 35

ACCOUNTABILITY IS THE SECRET TOOL THAT WILL HELP YOU ACHIEVE YOUR GOALS

*A*ccountability is the concept of accounting for your actions and being responsible for them. You can be accountable to a number of outside sources, as well as to yourself. As a personal coach, I work as an accountability partner. I help my clients and members achieve their goals and live a life filled with the benefits one gets when living an *Intentional Life*. This idea has great potential when it comes to keeping your procrastination in check.

When you are checking in with an accountability partner, you are holding yourself accountable to the action steps you've developed, and it gives more meaning to your tasks and makes accomplishing them in a timely manner more purposeful. Accountability may just be the secret tool you need to stop you from procrastinating.

Accountability requires answering to someone with regard to your accomplishments. When you have a task to complete, whether it's a small one or a more involved job, knowing you have to account for your results will provide more motivation to push forward through the rough parts. When I quit smoking, I took a cessation class and became accountable to the other thirteen men and women in the room. Even though they were strangers, it was important to me that I keep my word to refrain from smoking until the next class, and I did. On September 11, 1991, at 4:45 PM Pacific time, I had my last cigarette. I gave up a habit of nearly twenty years. It was one of the most difficult goals I had, but I continue to celebrate being a nonsmoker and remind myself of the achievement when I have tough times pursuing my other goals.

I learned a lot from each attempt I made over the years to quit smoking. It was ultimately more difficult to cut down than to quit cold turkey. When making a commitment to change a habit, it's easier to go "all in" than to just put your foot in the water to test the temperature. If you make a decision to accomplish a goal, my advice is to go "all in" and commit 100% to the goal. Make a decision and stick to it; this applies to goal setting, weight loss, drinking alcohol, complaining, or anything else you want to achieve. As the Nike commercials told us, "Just do it!"

Ultimately, you must be accountable to yourself, even if the task is one that has been assigned by someone else like a boss, teacher, or coach; the responsibility is yours and the consequences also fall on you. However, having an outside source to be accountable to can often be helpful to provide additional motivation for some of the more dreaded or mundane tasks; your accountability partner can help guide you in the right direction.

We procrastinate for a lot of reasons. Many are long-held habits or beliefs that exist within us, such as fear and self-doubt. Being a perfectionist has the power to hold you back...many perfectionists often use procrastination as a way of avoiding a task if they don't think it will be done perfectly. Ask me how I know!

While at other times, a task just seems too boring or inconsequential to deal with. However, most actions do come with a consequence if you fail to complete them, even if the cost is small. Having accountability can help you to avoid these consequences.

Being accountable means that you have someone to answer to if you fail to get something done. You are proactively taking responsibility for the task and know what the repercussions are if you fail to get it done. It can be a huge motivator to move you forward.

You can ensure you take personal responsibility by creating a to-do list by writing responsibilities down on your calendar and checking them off when you finish. I advise clients to concentrate on their Top 3. The Top 3 are the tasks that hold the greatest movement towards accomplishing your goals. One of the main features of concentrating on the Top 3 is that it starts with planning and setting goals.

We do this by identifying our Top 3 BIG Goals ("big rocks") for the year. When you start with the end in mind as Stephen Covey suggests, you can then analyze what steps must be taken to achieve those goals. I write the steps down and transfer them to my calendar; I cross off each as I make progress on the goal. This is a visual method to account for each completed duty, and it can be quite satisfying. If a task seems too large, my suggestion is to break it down even further into smaller steps and mark each one when completed.

Setting goals that are specific and measurable also increases accountability because doing so allows you to track your progress and to keep yourself on track. Enlisting the help of someone else can be a good strategy if you think you'll have trouble maintaining accountability on your own. Tell a trusted friend, family member, coach, or colleague about the action you'd like to take, and then ask them to check on you periodically to see how you're doing. Knowing you have to provide an update to an outside source can work wonders for your productivity. I find this to be true personally because I not only act as an accountability partner for clients and members of my coaching programs, but I also meet with my own mastermind group each week to share my personal and professional goals. Again, having outside sources to report to, brainstorm with, and celebrate accomplishments is inspiring and can motivate you to take additional actions and work toward other goals.

It's a great tool to be able to rely on accountability to help push you forward toward completing your to-do list. Members do this by developing small actionable steps that help them progress towards their goals; for example, Jean did this by making a plan to be accountable to living a healthier lifestyle when she stuck to her plan to monitor her water intake, get 10,000 steps per day, and change her food choices. She has celebrated the release of over 60 lbs. and continues on her personal health journey. Success stories like this make being an accountability partner a pure joy.

Having an accountability partner is a sure-fire way to ensure that you are fully responsible for the outcome of your actions. Holding yourself accountable really helps to make progress on your personal and professional goals. As an Achievement Coach, I want to see everyone live the life they create for themselves and enjoy the journey.

CHAPTER 36

ACCOUNTABILITY IS THE SECRET TOOL THAT WILL HELP YOU ACHIEVE YOUR GOALS JOURNAL ACTIVITY

*E*xercise from: Accountability IS the Secret Tool That Will Help You Achieve Your Goals

1. Do you have an accountability partner? How often do you meet?

---

2. Thinking with the *end in mind*, what are your Big 3 Goals and what are 3 steps you can do each day to help you move closer to achieving these goals?

----

3. What must you do to go "all in" to accomplish your goals?

~

CHAPTER 37

HOW TO UTILIZE BEHAVIOR-BASED GOALS

Setting goals simply works...and in the first month of my online coaching membership, *A Pilgrimage to Self*, members get access to the *Design an Intentional Life* workbook that helps them discover their goals in different areas of their lives. As discussed earlier, practicing self-awareness helps zero in on a focus goal and establish routines and habits that help you make those goals a reality.

I'll bet that the goals you currently want to achieve are based on a specific outcome, aren't they? These are called outcome-based goals, and they usually involve a change in a situation in our lives. A better job, more money, a bigger house, weight loss, and/or fitness... all of these are outcome-based goals, and these are what come to mind when most people think about goal setting.

But there is a different type of goal that doesn't focus on the outcome at all! Rather than focusing on the outcome, this type of goal focuses on changing behaviors that make achieving the outcome-based goals so much easier and faster! These types of goals are called behavior-based goals.

A Pilgrimage to Self helps women create the routines, rituals, and habits that become the foundation to achieving goals. It's important to create behavior-based goals to achieve the desired results you want to experience success.

With behavior-based goal setting, the intention is to create positive change in your habits, or behaviors, which will increase your chances of achieving your outcome-based goals. You can think of behavior-based goals as a midpoint, or stepping stone, on your way to your ideal outcome.

By creating and practicing positive habits until they become second nature, you increase the likelihood of achieving your end goals. But there is an unintended positive consequence of doing this! You see, while you're changing your behaviors, you'll also be utilizing those newly-cemented positive habits in many different areas of your life – some having nothing at all to do with your end goal! And this is the beauty of learning to utilize behavior-based goals alongside outcome-based goals.

The way my clients achieve their success is to create the larger outcome-based goal first. Then I ask them, "What positive habits will you need to create in order to increase your chances of achieving this goal?" The answer to that question will be your new behavior-based goals. Then, we put the Japanese technique of Kaizen into practice; remember, this involves taking small, continuous steps forward by taking those defined actions.

To demonstrate the technique here is an example.

Anna wants to lose thirty pounds. Losing weight is her larger, outcome-based goal. She knows that in order to lose the weight and keep it off, she needs to change habits that are preventing her right now from doing this. She sees that she needs to create new habits around consistency, discipline, and learning to not get overwhelmed.

Anna identifies these three new habits and finds techniques that she will implement to create positive habit changes that meet these interim behavior-based goals.

Designing and developing the action steps allow her to move forward; because she is following the philosophy of the Indian Proverb, *A House With Four Rooms* by doing something daily for her physical, mental, emotional, and spiritual well-being, she has established the appropriate routines and habits that move her closer to achieving her goal.

A few months later, Anna has lost thirty pounds but has also created stronger positive habits that will stay with her for the rest of her life. These new habits and confidence will allow Anna to design new personal and professional goals. She now can rely on this success to help build momentum towards her other goals.

CHAPTER 38

AIRING OUT MY ROOMS WITH LESSONS
FROM WINNIE THE POOH

"*W*e'll be Friends Forever, won't we, Pooh?' asked Piglet.

Even longer,' Pooh answered."

Winnie-the-Pooh

I often think about the lovable characters from one of my favorites in children's literature, A.A. Milne's *Winnie the Pooh*. As the mother of boys, I often read about Christopher Robin and his adventures with his favorite bear and their group of friends. Because Pooh Bear was one of my younger son's favorites, we watched Pooh videos over and over again. Have you ever had a song get stuck in your head? Well, for me, I often had (and still do) the words from Pooh's little exercise ditty, "Up down, touch the ground, puts me in the mood, for food." Pooh is proud of his round tummy, loves to indulge, and often overindulges in honey. And on one adventure, he even gets stuck in a doorway.

I've never been happy with my weight, but still, I love to indulge in the foods that make my taste buds dance: pasta, steak, comfort foods, desserts, and ice cream. The list goes on and on. My weight has gone up and down over the years, and as a young adult, I dealt with eating issues and controlled my weight by not indulging; I ate like a bird. Then I learned to take a different approach by eating sensibly and exercising regularly, and I learned physical goals are not reached overnight; they take time. As Christopher Robin explained when Pooh got stuck in the door, "Then there's only one thing to be done," he said. "We shall have to wait for you to get thin again." "How long does getting thin take?" asked Pooh anxiously. "About a week, I should think." So, as to not get "stuck" like Pooh, we should do something each day toward *airing* out our physical room; we can start by making healthier choices and behavioral changes that lead to a positive self-image.

Whenever I feel any type of anxiety or begin to question my abilities, I am encouraged by Christopher Robins' wise advice to Winnie the Pooh, "You are braver than you believe, stronger than you seem, and smarter than you think."

It's important that we monitor our self-talk for negative thoughts and ideas and be prepared to rephrase them for positive influences on desired outcomes. We have about 35-48 thoughts per minute, with an estimated 50,000 - 70,000 thoughts per day. That's a lot of power behind what motivates us and leads to the outcomes of our lives.

When I think about learning something new, designing a new project, or writing a new project, I often have to capture the thoughts that say, "You can't do that," or "You'll be judged by what you do or don't do." I think about that and reframe my thoughts. I think about other times that I have been successful and have overcome obstacles and challenges; these are times that I've been *braver, stronger,* and *smarter* than I thought I was in that moment of negative thinking. It's important to know the power behind all our thoughts because thoughts lead to actions. So if thoughts create our lives, think the good ones!

A House With Four Rooms is about making yourself a priority and living a complete life. Eating well, exercising our bodies, and monitoring our thoughts are foundational to self-care and living a balanced life. It is also important to have quality time for oneself and a higher power. This can be done through meditation, prayer, and relaxation.

A.A. Milne offers more advice, "Don't underestimate the value of doing nothing, of just going along, listening to all the things you can't hear, and not bothering." Being still and listening for the God whispers may take some practice, but once you incorporate this practice into your life, you will reap the benefits. Meditation is a great practice and reinforces the skills we need to cope with adversities, conflicts, and confusion. Meditation helps create the balance we need to live a complete life, as described in the Indian Proverb. Through meditation, we *air* out many rooms at one time. Meditation and prayer also allow us the opportunity to connect with a higher power. It's important to me that my day begins and ends in prayer; I turn to prayer several times throughout my day. The prayer I say often is "Thank You, God."

Connecting to others is important. Taking time to be with friends and family is valuable under positive and loving conditions. It is fun to participate in group activities that enrich our life experiences and provide love and support to our emotional health. Some of our actions may also help us *air* out several of our rooms. I know that when I meet others for a hike, game night, or dinner, I get the opportunity to *air* my rooms. I have been blessed to have people that have crossed my path, and just by knowing them, my heart sings. Again from A. A. Milne, "How lucky I am to have something that makes saying goodbyes so hard." Connecting to others and doing things we love, even our jobs, provides the excitement and desire to do it more...wow...magic!

Just as important to connecting to others, we must connect to ourselves. People may come and go in our lives, but we are always there, so it is essential that we become our own friends...best friends. We need to practice self-care; this practice must become a ritual and be authentic. Becoming your own best friend will be the longest relationship you'll ever have...fall in love with yourself. "How do you spell 'love'?' Piglet asked. Pooh responds, 'You don't spell it...you feel it.'" What should you be doing to connect with yourself? What must you do to feel *love*, know *love*, and be *love?* Do it...make it a practice by beginning with yourself and then reaching out to others.

It's important to be yourself, and as leadership speaker Steve Maroboli says, "When you are living the best version of yourself, you inspire others to live the best versions of themselves."

And in Tigger's words, "The wonderful thing about tiggers/ Is tiggers are wonderful things/ Their tops are made out of rubber/ Their bottoms are made out of springs/ They're bouncy, trouncy, flouncy, pouncy, fun, fun, fun, fun,fun/ But the most wonderful thing about tiggers is I'm the only one/ IIII'm the only one!"

We can learn a lot from Tigger, but the other characters also teach us. For example, the nature of Eeyore, the pessimistic, depressed donkey, shares his gloomy insights with the rest of the characters. Eeyore has a laundry list of things that cause him grief, and he carries these from place to place as he mopes around. Eeyore is certainly a contrast to Tigger. I might not be "up" all the time like Tigger, and I may have my Eeyore moments, but overall, I feel blessed that I'm excited about life and filled with gratitude. I also recognize that happiness is an "inside job," and we can choose how we respond to outside circumstances. So when I look at my day, I'd much rather be a Tigger than an Eeyore. "'What day is it?' asked Pooh. 'It's today,' squeaked Piglet. 'My favorite day,' said Pooh." This brings me to one last question: How about you...*Are you a Tigger or an Eeyore?*

CHAPTER 39

AIRING OUT MY ROOMS WITH LESSONS
FROM WINNIE THE POOH JOURNAL ACTIVITY

*E*xercise from: Airing out my rooms with lessons from Winnie the Pooh.

1. *Are you a Tigger or an Eeyore?*

~

CHAPTER 40

MIND, HEART, BODY, AND SPIRIT - THEY'RE ALL CONNECTED

*B*eing tired is generally considered a physical thing. A weary body is natural for someone who works hard physically or is aging. Most people don't know that the mind and the spirit are intricately connected to the body and can influence its health and vitality. Interesting enough, sometimes an illness or injury in the body is actually a manifestation of the mind or weariness of the spirit.

You are a spirit who has a mind and lives in a body. This is a simple and precise way of looking at the connection. Having a healthy mind and spirit can ensure the health of the heart and body. Likewise, having an unhealthy body can impact the health of the mind and spirit. *They are all intertwined.*

Remember, the philosophy of the Indian Proverb, *A House With Four Rooms* is to do something daily for your physical, mental, emotional, and spiritual well-being. This is important because what you think about, feel, and do influence your experiences.

Let's take a look.

Worry begins in the mind and expresses itself in the body: Worries are cerebral but they act out in aches, pains, and worse. Worrying over something begins in the mind and eventually manifests in issues like:

- Skin irritations
- Stomach and digestive troubles
- Anxiety - rapid heart rate, breathing issues
- Insomnia
- Muscle aches
- And more

As the mind works overtime, the body begins to express the pain, fear, and worry outward in multiple ways. Having been a chronic worrier, I believe that those thoughts were manifested in my body; even now, I'm aware of my thoughts and what's going on with my body because my life depends on it.

A grieved spirit can cause mental health issues: Not all mental health symptoms come from organic mental illness. Some mental health issues like situational depression, anxiety, and some personality disorders can come from traumatic experiences, loss, or a sense of disconnection. Being weary in your spirit can lead to issues in the mind that impede normal functioning.

Developing my Forgiveness and Gratitude practices was essential for my spiritual well-being and became a key component of my coaching programs. When something makes a significant difference to living an *Intentional Life,* it's important to adopt it as a routine, ritual, or habit.

A chronic disease or illness can impact the mind and the spirit: Sometimes the body doesn't function well. An illness, disease, injury, or defect can create pain or challenges that affect our mental health. Being chronically ill or living with the effects of a disease or defect can elevate mental health issues like depression or anxiety.

You are a spirit who has a mind and lives in a body. The three are connected and impact one another. Being weary in any one area can wear you out in other areas of your life. Acknowledging your need for rest as a preventative tool *and* a restorative tool matters. A common analogy is an idea of lining up dominoes in such a way that when setting up, once one is knocked over, it knocks all the others over in the lineup.

When you practice self-care and are willing to rest your mind, heart, body, or spirit, you help maximize your day-to-day life and give yourself the energy to meet your commitments. Get in tune with your mind, heart, body, and spirit connection so you can identify where you are tired and take the necessary steps to rejuvenate. Remember, small steps forward are still forward progress...learn to be self-aware and observe your mind, heart, body, and spirit.

CHAPTER 41

YOUR TURN TO REVIEW YOUR LIFE

*T*he process of slow thinking is about being in a great mental space to review or really look at your current life. It's a good idea to frequently examine all the different areas that make up your life - like your job, your business, your hobbies, your family, and your relationships. What's working and what isn't? Are you as happy as you'd like to be?

If you don't take the time to reflect and imagine what could be, you won't change and grow. Your personal development and growth depend on it! This is why my coaching programs start on the PATHS of Self-Awareness and Goal Setting. We learn that it's important to set aside some time each week to examine the different areas of our lives and really think about what we want in the long run. Managing your time and activities is key to living an *Intentional Life*. Your life depends on it!

Let's start by discussing your job or what you do for a living. You spend a good chunk of your waking hours doing something to pay the bills. Is it what you want to do? Do you enjoy it? I'm not talking about the occasional bad day or those annoying tasks each job brings with them, but overall job satisfaction. We all have those days; however, if you're not happy doing what you're doing, it may be time to think about doing something else. It may be time to reevaluate your career goals.

It's not unusual to learn that many of my clients feel like they've gone to college and trained for a specific career only to discover that career choice doesn't bring them joy. It takes courage, faith, and belief in self to make a different choice. When you think about your job, take some time to contemplate your salary and benefits as well. Is there room for improvement? What can you do to increase your chances for advancement or a raise? What could you do to achieve career satisfaction? If you're not going to take responsibility for your own career, who will?

You may think that this doesn't apply to you, and maybe you're right. But for many of us, in this gig economy we've come to live in, keeping our job has become a business. We are the CEO of our own career and need to take an active role in finding the best options and negotiating the best deals...or maybe you're supplementing your income with a side hustle. Nothing wrong with that, but I'm sure it could benefit from some slow thinking that allows you to reflect on what is working and what may need to change. Or maybe you're trying to replace your day job with a business of your own. Good for you. Keep at it and make sure you're on the right track by taking the time to think strategically and set some goals for the near and far future. Invest your time, money, and energy into making those goals your reality.

Last but not least, take some time to review the various aspects of your personal life. What are you doing for your physical, mental, emotional, and spiritual wellbeing? What's working and what isn't? Are you living an *Intentional Life*? What relationships do you want to invest more time in, which would you be better off letting go? Think about the people closest to you. What can you do to become a better friend, spouse, or parent? We all have room for improvement here.

Taking the time to think about these things will make you a better person and hopefully a happier one as well.

This is so important to living your *Intentional Life*...and with this reflective process, you'll feel empowered and confident to move on and forward with clarity, purpose, and direction.

Many of the women I work with have often felt like their lives were at a DEAD END, but when they make the decision to work with me, they've realized that they are really at a CROSSROADS...they can pivot and take the journey to discover, design, and develop an *Intentional Life*. They take the first steps of the journey on the PATHS that move them on and forward with the next chapter of their lives...we use masterclasses on various topics, interviews with lifestyle experts, and practical, inspirational, and spiritual guidance provided in ebooks, workbooks, exercises, and Q & A sessions to help them engage in their own lives.

There is no reason not to engage in the events that will help you pivot from where you are now to where you'd like to go...imagine your best life and then take it from ordinary to extraordinary. Join like-minded people in activities that support your complete wellbeing.

It's wonderful to be a part of such encouraging and supportive communities. It's inspiring to see the positive impact on other women's lives because it can impact our own.

You can find supportive communities in your hometowns or with online groups. There are so many Facebook groups available, that you may want to do a quick search to find those that interest you.

Over the years, my community has grown with case studies, referrals, and testimonials. It's encouraging to be able to share success stories that illustrate the possibilities available to those that choose them. Stories help us understand what can be achieved by introducing us to others that have done what we wish to accomplish.

As a coach, it's always a pleasure to watch clients create *Intentional Lives*: Jean is on a health journey and has already lost 60 lbs., Donna went back to school after raising her grandsons and is now working her dream job, Jen wrote her first book, while Jane is awakening to her authentic self after ending a long marriage. What these women have in common is that they recognized they needed accountability and guidance so they took the first steps by committing to themselves. These women continue to move forward with the benefits of personal and professional development and are experiencing the joys of living their own *Intentional Lives*.

Are you ready to commit and invest in yourself? I hope so because your *Intentional Life* depends on it! My point is, make sure you are living your own *Intentional Life*...we get one life to live, so make it your BEST life!

~

CHAPTER 42

YOUR TURN TO REVIEW YOUR LIFE JOURNAL ACTIVITY

xercise from: Your Turn to Review YOUR Life

1. What is your current job and/or career field?

_____

_____

_____

_____

_____

_____

_____

_____

_____

_____

_____

_____

_____

_____

_____

_____

_____

2. What education and/or training do you currently have?

_____

_____

_____

_____

_____

_____

_____

_____

_____

_____

3. What do you like about your current work?

_____

_____

_____

_____

_____

_____

_____

_____

_____

_____

_____

_____

_____

_____

_____

_____

_____

_____

_____

_____

_____

4. Is there anything you would like to change about your work life, career field, or position?

5. What would you do for a job if you knew you could not fail?

----

6. What practices have you committed to for your physical, mental, emotional, and spiritual wellbeing?

---

7. Are you living an *Intentional Life*? In what ways?

----

8. Are there any changes you'd like to make to your life?

_____

_____

_____

_____

_____

_____

_____

_____

_____

_____

_____

_____

_____

_____

_____

_____

_____

_____

_____

9. What relationships do you want to invest more time in, which would you be better off letting go?

_____

_____

_____

_____

_____

_____

_____

_____

_____

_____

_____

_____

_____

_____

_____

_____

_____

_____

10. Think about the people closest to you. What can you do to become a better friend, spouse, or parent?

~

HOW DO YOU GET TO ACHIEVE
IT ALL?

The BIG Rock Theory is about identifying and scheduling your BIG rocks first; these are the most important things in your life that really matter.

In my example, by filling the vase with the larger rocks first, with a little jiggle, the smaller rocks will fill in the gaps, and then there is room available for the pebbles and sand.

The vase represents your life. How do you wish to fill it?

Just like your vase, you should fill your life with the most important things first; these are the things that will make the biggest difference in your life.

Keep in mind, if you fill the vase with the sand first, there is little space for the other rocks. As with life, by spending your time and energy on the small stuff like material things, you will never have room in your life for what really matters.

So, let's fill the vase with sand, pebbles, smaller rocks, and the BIG rocks in a way to have them all fit. This is the same way you would schedule your calendar for your life.

1. Identify and schedule your BIG Rocks first; these are the things that really matter: major goals, travel, important dates, family events, health, etc.

2. Then schedule (smaller rocks) routines; these are the other things in life that are essential: self-care practices, work, family, shopping, household responsibilities, etc.

3. Add the other things that matter, but on a smaller scale: (pebbles): your house, car, hobbies, etc.

4. The sand is everything else; it's the small stuff: TV, playing videos, searching the Internet, etc.

5. BONUS...I added a glass of water. After shifting the vase and allowing the rocks, pebbles, and sand to settle, you now have room to pour the water. The water washes over the stones and is absorbed by the sand.

What might the water represent in your life?

CHAPTER 43

SET BIG GOALS & REVIEW THEM REGULARLY

*G*oals and habits are closely related and dependent on each other. When you set goals, you're creating milestones to reach for by setting a tangible timeline for making your dreams come true. However, in order to attain those goals, you must reach certain objectives and take steps each day in order to obtain them. We use a process from the Japanese called Kaizen by making small consistent progress that helps one achieve their goals and live their *Intentional Lives*.

These steps you take are the routines, habits, or things you get used to doing repeatedly in order to attain the desired outcome. One of the strategies that works best to avoid *decision fatigue* is to purposefully make some of your daily decisions in advance. This works especially well when you think about what you'll eat for breakfast and lunch or what outfits you'll wear each day. The actions you take should purposefully move you forward to achieving the milestones and make the progress you want to accomplish and experience.

Setting goals and reviewing them on a regular basis is also a habit. Goal setting is such an important habit to develop and it can impact your life. You don't have to wait until the new year or the beginning of a new month to get started. There's no better time than right now. Making a commitment to "airing out" your four rooms daily and following through becomes the foundation for every area of your life. You become stronger and can rely on your confidence, routines, and experiences to help you push forward to achieve your heart's desire.

Goals give you direction for your life, especially when they align with your purpose. When you decide you'd like to achieve something, whether it's big or small, you have a destination, and you know in which direction you wish to move. A life without goals is often lived on autopilot. You'll find yourself doing what you have to do in order to make it through each day, rather than striving to make intentional choices that reflect your values and priorities. Living an *Intentional Life* is about having goals that provide structure to a hectic life.

Setting goals helps you to see what's important in your life. Doing so also improves your decision-making. When you know what you want to accomplish over a given period of time, you will base your decisions and your actions on finding ways to make that happen. You'll discover your choices are more intentional and purposeful, not just random and impulsive. You'll set up routines that spill over into every area of your life.

Even when you don't set clear and concise goals, it's likely that you have an idea of what you want in life. However, staying focused enough to see the process through to completion is difficult without getting into the habit of setting real, tangible goals, and reviewing them on a regular basis to be sure you're still on track. As they say, a goal without a plan is just a wish. Wishing isn't usually enough to make things happen, but the process of setting intentional goals helps you to stay focused and on target. That's why focusing on your Top 3 is successful; you make continued progress to reach your goals.

When you set a specific goal (your "big rock"), you know what it is that you want. Your desire is no longer vague and you are ready for the next step. Proper goal setting involves creating a game plan for how you'll reach the finish line. As an Achievement Coach, I've come up with systems that help you determine what steps you need to take and how to develop a timeline for achieving your ultimate goal. This gives you the motivation to keep going even when things are hard and increases your chance of ultimate success.

Getting into the habit of setting goals puts you in charge of your life, rather than just going with the flow and hoping for the best...with a wish and a prayer. My prayer partner, Jim, used to remind me that we must put feet on our prayers to accomplish what we want.

One of the steps you can take to put "feet" on your prayers, goals, and dreams is to sit down and set a few realistic goals for yourself, and you'll start to notice these benefits. Soon, goal setting will become a habit you rely on. I've long believed in the power of everyday routines, rituals, and habits because of my experience living the philosophy of *A House With Four Rooms* by committing to do something daily for my physical, mental, emotional, and spiritual well-being.

Imagine, what would your life look like if you implemented a new routine each week for a year?

CHAPTER 44

SET BIG GOALS & REVIEW THEM REGULARLY
JOURNAL ACTIVITY

*E*xercise from: Set Big Goals & Review Them Regularly

1. Take the time to schedule your "big rocks" on a yearly calendar. Your "big rocks" are those activities, events, and experiences that have the most meaning for you, may require many steps to achieve, and are essential to your Intentional Life. What are some of your "big rocks"?

-
-
-
-
-
-
-
-

2. Working with the *end in mind*, what are some of the stepping stones, or rocks that will help you to achieve your "big rock" experiences? Add them to your calendar.

-
-
-
-
-
-
-
-
-
-
-
-
-
-
-
-
-

3. Now identify the smaller rocks that must be completed for your daily life. Remember to include activities for your physical, mental, emotional, and spiritual wellbeing. Block out time on your calendar.

-
-
-
-
-
-
-
-
-
-
-
-
-
-
-
-
-
-
-

4. Divide your calendar into quarters and identify your "Big 3" Goals for each quarter?

January to March

-
-
-

April to June

-
-
-

July to September

-
-
-

October to December

-
-
-

5. Add weekly or monthly accountability check-in dates to review your actions and plans. This is an opportunity to adjust your calendar to help you make progress on all of your goals. Sunday evening is often a good time to look at the week ahead, identify and align your daily and weekly "Top 3" goals, make appropriate decisions to avoid decision fatigue, and include intentional activities that support your complete wellbeing. What intentional activities are important to your success?

-
-
-
-
-
-
-
-
-
-

6. Download your gift copy of The Power of Every Day Routines at https://www.lisamcgrath.me/offers/YUFefz2S to learn additional strategies for "airing" your physical, mental, emotional, and spiritual rooms and implementing new routines into your daily life.

∾

CHAPTER 45

YOUR PURPOSE MAY EVOLVE AND CHANGE
AS YOU DO... AND THAT'S OKAY

J'm sure throughout this book you've been thinking a lot about living with purpose and what that means to you right now. Hopefully, you're living more intentionally already and are changing things here and there to better align with your purpose. You may even discover your big passion and your calling and work towards making that happen. That's great, but there's something we haven't talked about much. It's that we all grow and change as time goes by. And with that, our purposes change. I know I've had my life change several times through life circumstances: homelessness, marriage, divorce, family dysfunction and addictions, an empty nest, job changes, moving from state to state and out of the country, entrepreneurship, and contemplating retirement. Life changes and so does our purpose, and that's okay.

Let's say you're a mother of small children. Right now, living with purpose may mean spending as much time as possible raising your kids. That may mean becoming a stay-at-home mom, working only part-time, or working from home. That's great, but don't feel like that can't change as time goes by. A few years from now, the kids will all be in school and then in time, you'll find you have an empty nest...you find yourself with even more time on your hands. It's perfectly fine to switch focus and get back into your career or try something completely new. Things change and evolve. You change and evolve. Your purpose may evolve as well and that's perfectly normal and how it should be.

That's why it's a good idea to occasionally take some time and think about what's important to you and make sure you're still living a purpose-driven life based on your *current values* and ideas. It's okay to change and adjust if things no longer feel like a good fit. While it's something you can do "on the fly" as you move through your days and weeks, it can also be helpful to stop every few months and take time to really think about reevaluating your life, your goals, and your circumstances.

Reflection and questioning are a major part of my coaching programs that take members on a sacred journey to Discover, Design, and Develop their own *Intentional Life*.

As humans, we are creatures of habit and will often stick to a plan, an idea, or a routine because that's how we've always done it, or out of a desire to tough it out. While that's admirable and there's certainly a time and place for this, it's also good to take some time to reflect and second guess what you're doing. You don't want to find yourself in a rut...I used to describe this feeling as "being sick and tired of being sick and tired."

You want to live your life intentionally and with purpose. That means you should always second guess yourself and make sure what you're doing is a good fit and the best way to live purposefully. If it is, great... carry on. If it isn't, it's time to pivot and make some changes until what you do aligns with your purposes.

Living an *Intentional Life* begins with finding your way back to yourself for reasons such as overwhelm, burnout, or midlife crisis. The journey starts with self-awareness as you discover your current mindset, core beliefs, and negative self-talk.

Make sure to visit each of your four rooms to "air" them out and work toward a focus goal. Some women decide to focus on health and weight issues, while others may focus on becoming debt-free or decluttering their personal space and minds. As your personal journey continues, you'll learn strategies and practices that will move you along the PATHS toward self-love, purpose and meaning, and living an extraordinary life.

Don't you deserve to feel peace, joy, and success every single day? Of course, you do.

There are many ways to start your journey of personal and professional development: implement what you've learned from reading, taking courses, therapy, and counseling. You can find an accountability partner or group or hire a coach.

If you are interested in learning more about my programs, visit my website at https://www.lisamcgrath.me.

Besides private coaching, I also have the monthly membership *A Pilgrimage to Self* that has been described in the chapters and journal activities within this book.

The membership has been developed for those women that want to learn strategies and systems to make life easier, more joyful, and intentional. The monthly masterclasses, videos, and lessons are made available each week to avoid overwhelm, and when you take the time to do the exercises and implement what you learn, your life transforms and you find yourself living with boundaries, self-love, and more confidence.

The online membership is designed for women wanting to take the transformation journey at a regular pace, one stepping stone at a time. It is an independent program for those committed to themselves, their goals, and their journey.

For acceleration, and for busy individuals, especially entrepreneurs, the Achieve with UNLIMITED Laser Coaching is a great program.

This program works because we stick with an agenda and it's individualized to you. Here's how it works:

1. You join for the monthly, 6 months, or yearly plan.
2. You'll get an email from me with a link to my calendar so we can have our first coaching session.
3. Your first call is 30 minutes to make sure the coaching is perfect for you. We'll come up with a custom plan to help you focus, accelerate, and progress towards your goals.
4. At the end of our call, and each call thereafter, we'll agree on your next best ACTION STEPS (homework) that will move you forward and keep you accountable.
5. Once your homework is complete, you can schedule your next 15-minute call.

For example, have your coaching session on a Wednesday, do your homework right after the call, and you can schedule your next call that very same day. Truly Unlimited Coaching!

And don't worry, if you get stuck on the homework or need support between calls, I'm just an email away.

Both men and women have found this accelerated plan beneficial because they focus on particular goals, practice Kaizen, have me as an accountability partner, and truly make progress on living their *Intentional Life*. Image what your life would be like in three months, six months, or a year from now if you took action to achieve your personal and professional goals.

Another major benefit of the Achieve with UNLIMITED Laser Coaching program is that clients understand their own responsibility for making things happen. They make goals, complete actions steps, celebrate wins, and make sure their intentional actions align with their purpose. It's remarkable, and as their Achievement Coach, I'm honored to witness their successes.

All of my coaching programs follow the philosophy of the Indian Proverb *A House With Four Rooms* because when we are building our lives on a solid foundation of physical, mental, emotional, and spiritual wellbeing, we are empowered to achieve in every area of our lives.

~

CHAPTER 46

NEXT STEPS...

*I*f you haven't downloaded my gift of *The Power of Every Day Routines*, please go to https://www.lisamcgrath.me/offers/YUFefz2S for your free copy.

Take the time to be reflective as you work through the journaling prompts and exercises.

This process has been successful for hundreds of others on their personal journeys to discover, design, and develop their *Intentional Lives*. By following the simple philosophy of *A House With Four Rooms*, they build a life with complete well-being, fantastic opportunities, and personal and professional success.

To learn more about my programs, visit my website at https://www.lisamcgrath.me.

ACKNOWLEDGMENTS

I'm profoundly grateful for finding Rumer Godden's mention of the Indian Proverb *A House with Four Rooms* early in my life. It is the foundation of my life and coaching business.

Thanks to Scott Vandiver for his support, encouragement, and patience. To friends and family within my inner circle, I offer my sincere appreciation for enriching my life.

I'm grateful for my first mentors and coaches: Wayne Dyer, Louise Hay, and Cheryl Richardson. And to those that have helped me continue my journey: Paul and Melissa Pruitt, Forbes Riley, Christian Mickelsen, Stu McLaren, Amy Porterfield, Jeff Walker, Mel Robbins, Rob Goyette, Donna Kozik, Chris Winfield, and Jen Gottlieb.

My sincere thanks to those that have sent comforting prayers, messages, cards, and condolences with my son's passing from Covid-19. The grieving process is difficult, but my faith and life practices are grounded in the philosophy of *A House With Four Rooms.*

~

ABOUT THE AUTHOR

Meet Lisa McGrath, America's Achievement Coach...international bestselling author, speaker, teacher, and accountability partner. Lisa's search for a deeper meaning and purpose began as a little girl because she was thrust into adulthood early. She lived on her own and sought out ways *of living a more meaningful life.* A spiritual calling led her on a journey of healing and purpose.

She learned that we ALL have stories, but sometimes we don't feel like we have a voice. As America's Achievement Coach, she helps others, especially entrepreneurs, coaches, and aspiring authors like herself, craft their stories that help heal, inspire, and support others. Participants in her *Writing, Publishing, and Marketing* course have the opportunity to submit their stories for the international bestselling anthology *Pages with Purpose* that helps the authors gain visibility, authority, and credibility.

Her programs include the exclusive *Achieve with UNLIMITED Laser Coaching* for busy individuals that want to accelerate their journey and accomplish their personal and professional goals, private 1:1 coaching for life and business, and online membership, *A Pilgrimage to Self*, for women to learn and follow the PATHS of Living an *Intentional Life*.

With a firm belief in personal and professional development, she continues her growth journey with coaches that include Paul and Melissa Pruitt, Forbes Riley, Christian Mickelsen, Stu McLaren, Amy Porterfield, Jeff Walker, Mel Robbins, Rob Goyette, Donna Kozik, Chris Winfield, and Jen Gottlieb. Her mentors also include Wayne Dyer, Louise Hay, and Cheryl Richardson.

Her formal education includes a Masters in Liberal Arts and degrees in English, Art History, and Teaching and the professional distinction of National Board Certified Teacher. Her further studies include certification in Neuro-linguistic programming, EFT Tapping, Ho'oponopono, Kaizen, The Law of Attraction, Cognitive-Behavior Therapy, and Positive Psychology.

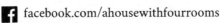

facebook.com/ahousewithfourrooms
twitter.com/1lisamcgrath
instagram.com/coachlisamcgrath
linkedin.com/in/coachlisamcgrath

Made in the USA
Middletown, DE
02 February 2022

60274738R00136